Journey Into Wholeness

A Map for Living Life Fully

Annaliese Kohinoor-Hagan
and
Ariana Khent

**Published by
Hara Publishing
P.O. Box 19732
Seattle, WA 98109**

Copyright 1997 by Annaliese Kohinoor-Hagan
and Ariana Khent

ISBN: 1-883697-13-1

Library of Congress Catalog Card Number:
96-78298

Manufactured in the United States
10 9 8 7 6 5 4 3 2

Grateful acknowledgment is made for permission granted by Henry Holt and Company, Inc. for portions reprinted from THE FORGOTTEN LANGUAGE by Erich Fromm, copyright 1951 by Erich Fromm; and by HarperCollins Publishers, Inc. for portions reprinted from A RETURN TO LOVE by Marianne Williamson, copyright 1992 by Marianne Williamson.

Cover Design: Stephen Peringer and Ron deWilde
Desktop Publishers: Eric Mead and Shael Anderson
Supervising Editor: Vicki McCown

DEDICATED WITH GREAT LOVE TO OUR TEACHERS

ACKNOWLEDGMENTS
Our heartfelt thanks

—

To Dave Hagan, our "knight in shining armor," for his support and guidance.

To our families and friends for their faith and support.

To the following brave souls who read our manuscript and offered their valuable insights: Alecia Anderson, Andrew Stevens, Carol Wayne, Caitanya, Dee Ruzicka, Loretta Granatelli, Roxee Hatfield, Tammy Kasprowicz, Terry Latshaw, Tess Rolfe, Traci Russell-Calderon, Verla Wade, Yunya Hauth.

To Sheryn Hara, who took us under her publishing wing.

To Stephen Peringer, for his artistic genius.

To Bob Bratt, our computer guru.

To Suki, our cosmic timekeeper.

Contents

INTRODUCTION

Greetings. It is our honor to share this information with you. Before we start, we would like to introduce ourselves by sharing a bit of our journey with you.

The two of us have very similar backgrounds. We both grew up in the Pacific Northwest in traditional home environments. We led what would be considered very ordinary lives in our lower/middle-class, Protestant, American surroundings. We both have spent the past several years working in the adult education and social service fields.

In our mid-twenties we each began to question the traditional values that had permeated our lives, and set out on a long search for The Truth. Our independent searches included extensive reading and participation in countless workshops, seminars, and retreats. We have studied and experienced a wide variety of spiritual paths including many of the world's major religions. Along the way we encountered New Age and new thought, as well as the ancient and arcane teachings. In our individual seeking, we found many extraordinary ways of approaching life. Ultimately, in our quest for The Truth, we found that truth has many faces and can appear different for each one of us. Truth is a unique, experiential and personal knowing that is felt within the core of our beings. So we bring you our Truths as we have embraced them.

As a result of our extensive explorations we have come to recognize a new energy, a powerful way to journey through life that is available to all! We are living in a time of powerful change. There is a new way to *be* which provides us with unprecedented ease in life. Time itself seems to be accelerating as our life's lessons appear to us in much quicker succession, with less and less breathing room in between. There is an enhanced ability to love and be loved. Each day offers the potential for more passion, excitement and fulfillment. Grace pours abundantly through all of our lives. We have only to open our eyes of awareness to witness it. As we do, each day becomes richer.

We think of ourselves as being quite ordinary people who simply have a deep yearning for more in life. Like everyone, we have had (and continue to have) both joyful and challenging journeys along life's paths. In our individual experiences we have undergone great pain, known abundant joy, endured debilitating fear and savored boundless love. We continue to experience challenges, but underlying the challenges is a pervasive feeling of joy that fills each moment! Joy is our natural state. Our lives are magical as we live them now. It brings us great pleasure to share this magic with you. The journey through life is meant to be joyous, love-filled, abundant, serene and graced with a sense of power and mastery, not misery. This is what we call "wholeness." It is our birthright to live in the state of wholeness that is life's intended gift for each and every one of us.

All that may be standing between wholeness and the magic it brings is the thinnest of veils. *Journey Into Wholeness* is our offering to you to assist you in removing any remaining obstacles that may be obscuring the joy and magic that is rightfully yours.

We use the word "journey" as a metaphor describing life in all of its many aspects, including the quest for finding purpose and meaning. All of the events in our lives, whether we judge them as positive or negative, have purpose, and exist in harmony with life's unfolding. The word "wholeness" denotes the oneness, harmony, balance and unity that is inherent in our nature. Living in the wholeness of our personal journeys allows us to live life to its richest and fullest potential.

This book is a map of our experiences and is by no means the absolute truth. We ask you to take the information offered here and make it your own. To accomplish this, we suggest that you turn the knowledge that is found within these pages into personal wisdom. We define knowledge as an accumulation of facts and information. Our awareness and consciousness holds knowledge in the form of good ideas. It is static and powerless when it is not put to use. Knowledge becomes powerful only when we transform it into wisdom. Wisdom is knowledge put into action. We give our personal storehouse of knowledge power by living what we know—transforming it into wisdom or action. Knowledge becomes wisdom when we put our good ideas into meaningful action in our lives.

As in any journey, it is up to each one of us to find our own direction. We each have preferences and priorities that take precedent in determining our way. This is as it should be. We entreat you to use your intrinsic inner knowing as your compass in determining which directions you take as you set out on your journey into wholeness. You are very special and unique, and you have your own way of experiencing your world.

This is a book for anyone who has ever doubted themselves and their ability to create the experience of life they want. *Journey Into Wholeness* is about self-empowerment. By self-empowerment we do not mean power over others, but rather power that uncovers and develops our innate abilities and strengths. *Journey Into Wholeness* presents an opportunity to reveal our light: the beauty, grace, love, peace and power that lives within us. This *is* who we are. When we uncover that truth it sets us free.

The information we bring has not always come easily over the years. Our wish for you is that your journey will go smoothly and without the effort and struggle that we have experienced. We bring you our insights and learnings with great love. Do with it as you wish for now it is yours. We will be with you in spirit. May your journey be joyous and magnificent every step of the way!

BE AT PEACE

FOR YOU ARE GREATLY LOVED

Annaliese Kohinoor-Hagan and Ariana Khent

1

THE JOURNEY BEGINS...

Our deepest fear is not that we are inadequate. Our deepest fear is that we are powerful beyond measure. It is our light, not our darkness, that most frightens us. We ask ourselves, Who am I to be brilliant, gorgeous, talented and fabulous? Actually, who are you not to be? You are a child of God. Your playing small doesn't serve the world. There's nothing enlightened about shrinking so that other people won't feel insecure around you.... We were born to make manifest the glory of God that is within us. It's not just in some of us; it's in everyone. And as we let our own light shine, we unconsciously give other people permission to do the same. As we are liberated from our own fear, our presence automatically liberates others.

Written by Marianne Williamson, *A Return to Love*
Quoted in the 1994 inaugural speech of
President Nelson Mandela

Where Does This Journey Lead?

The journey you are about to undertake is a personal odyssey of reclaiming your True Self. You are already whole and complete. The purpose of this particular journey is to recognize and embrace your intrinsic wholeness and express more fully the Truth of who you are. This is not a course in self-improvement, but rather a process of uncovering and releasing the profound power that lives silently within you. This power *is* you and has been patiently waiting for its full unfolding. To reside in the potency of this power requires embarking upon an inner exploration—an internal journey.

Why would we embark upon this journey into wholeness? Can we look forward to arriving *somewhere* and stopping at our journey's end? What is the final destination? Ultimately there is no final destination, only the ongoing journey of life. There is truth to the saying, "Life is not a destination but a journey." We journey into wholeness to enhance the *quality* of our experiences along the way. Every experience becomes part of life's journey and is appropriate. Does this mean that change is unnecessary? Probably not. All of our experiences offer the gift of increased awareness and are the seeds for expansiveness. Our journeys are ongong into forever. Such is our nature.

Evaluating the Quality of Our Lives

It is advantageous to slow down now and then and evaluate the components which give purpose and meaning to our lives. There are many areas of life that create an impact on our level of fulfillment. Let us evaluate a few of the areas which affect our ability to experience wholeness by asking the following questions:

Do I operate from confusion or clarity?

As we walk in wholeness, we possess *clarity* and proceed in the light of awareness rather that groping blindly in the dark. Our intuitive, right brain provides information and ideas for optimum guidance. The left brain's reasoning capabilities support us in following our intuitive guidance. When we approach one of life's crossroads where a choice must be made, we are attentive to the "sign posts" provided by our intuitive and logical minds which lead us to the fulfillment of our dreams.

Do I feel capable of handling whatever life presents?

Our *power* radiates from within. In our wholeness we feel capable of effectively managing life's challenges. A sense of empowerment fills us as energy flows unimpeded throughout our bodies, allowing us to move through difficulties and stress. In the face of adversity or change, we no longer feel helpless or stuck. We take responsibility for what we create, knowing we have the resources to create different outcomes if we choose.

Am I fully aware of the beliefs which run my life and do they support me?

Beliefs are the foundation upon which the experiences of life are built. Our endeavors are successful or unsuccessful depending upon our beliefs. Living in wholeness, we effectively identify and release the beliefs and behavior patterns that no longer reflect our best interest. As we adopt empowering beliefs, we realize our dreams, goals and desires.

Am I hard on myself?

Self-acceptance is the capacity to be compassionate with ourselves. Our wholeness allows us to accept and recognize all aspects of ourselves, both positive and the negative. In this allowance we are able to move forward in life without settling into complacency, no longer filtering our decisions through fear, doubt and anger.

Am I having fun yet?

We relax into the present moment as we experience wholeness. Our lives are enriched with *enjoyment*, fun and laughter. Our serious side takes a back seat and we lighten up. When we began writing this book, we climbed a mountain behind Annaliese's home, intending to spend several hours seriously getting organized with our writing. Annaliese's dog, Suki, accompanied us on this venture and had other plans. She kicked dirt all over us and our blanket, chewed and pulled at our clothes and sat in the middle of our writing materials. Since she had never behaved in this manner, we decided we had better stop and pay attention to her "message." We took a few moments to focus inward and discovered that we were taking this whole writing project too seriously and needed to lighten up and have fun! We intuited we were to write only two hours a day. Suki seemed to know this because over the ensuing months she let us know when our two-hour time limit was up!

How well do I take care of my body?

Our bodies are the vehicles through which we experience life. The well-being of our bodies is given top priority as we honor our wholeness. We pay attention to the messages of our bodies and take actions which support their *health*. Accepting our feelings and emotions is a vital contributor to our overall well-being.

Can I remove my "Lone Ranger" mask and ask for support?

When we honor our wholeness, we reach out for *support*. We know we do not have to venture forth alone. We recognize our need for assistance and request it, knowing that our request is a sign of strength, not weakness. Receiving support does not mean that we are dependent on others. Our personal effectiveness is enriched by enlisting the aid of others. Support enriches our lives with strength, companionship and communion of spirit.

Do I celebrate myself?

We proclaim our wholeness as we celebrate and *honor* the passages of our lives. We realize the moments of our lives are precious and that our life experiences are sacred. We express this understanding through special ceremony and celebration and taking the time to mark our transitions in a spirit of honor and love.

Am I excited about life?

In our wholeness, we follow our hearts' desires with *passion* and purpose. Our creativity quotient is high. We arise each morning with confident expectation for the day, looking forward to what awaits us. Our hearts sing and we respond with spontaneity, creativity and playfulness in each moment. Our work becomes play.

There is only one important question to ask when such an evaluation is made: "Do all elements of my life define who I am and what is most important to me?" If an unequivocal

"Yes!" is your response, it is obvious that you are on a course that serves you well. If, however, your answer is "No," and you experience a sense of confusion or doubt, this may indicate that a change in direction is needed. Changing directions does not necessarily mean a physical change. The experience of our lives is most strongly affected by the beliefs we hold, as we will explore in the next chapter.

Every journey into wholeness includes both challenge and ease—light and dark. We attain new heights by exploring the entire range of human experiences—in particular the challenges that accompany change. Challenge and change seem to go hand in hand. Let us explore the realm of challenge, change and chaos.

Change In Life / Chaos

Before the beginning of great brilliance..., there must be chaos. Before a brilliant person begins something great, they must look foolish to the crowd.

From the *I Ching*

Chaos is part of the expansion process. When life feels like it's falling down around your knees, you think you are not getting it, you feel like you are messing up and your shortcomings are blatantly in your face, CONGRATULATIONS!!!! Change is at hand! These misgivings indicate that you are on the brink of change and growth.

In 1977, Belgian physicist, Ilya Prigonine, won a Nobel Prize for his theory of "Dissipative Structures"—a chaos theory. He suggested that a period of dissolution—passing, demise, extinction, disintegration, falling apart—must occur before any social or human system can progress into a higher level of organization or existence. His theory is referred to as the "Chaos Theory."

As we move farther along in our journeys into wholeness, fear, doubt, and self-judgment can easily dominate during periods of restructuring. We are literally moving beyond the comfort zone, and being uncomfortable is part of the process! The sense of falling apart is a creative event as it makes room for newness and growth—darkness into light.

Periods of chaos, calamity and disorderliness are the precursors to the next stage of wholeness and renewal. Our ability to create newness in our lives comes from these times of challenge. We are invited to release old, unworkable patterns and behaviors and move into the next level of growth.

The following is a Sufi story illustrating how the elements of change, chaos and challenge manifested in one woman's life:

Fatima the Spinner and the Tent

Long ago there was a young woman named Fatima. Her father, a wealthy spinner, was going on a long journey to an island across the sea to conduct business. He asked Fatima to come with him, hoping she might find a husband along the way. However, the ship upon which they were sailing encountered a great storm and was crushed to pieces, killing the father. Fatima was washed up on the shore. A family of clothmakers found her suffering from exposure and with little memory of the past. They took her in and for the next two years she learned their trade.

One day a band of slave traders captured Fatima and took her to Istanbul, where she was sold as a slave. For the second time, her world had collapsed. The man who bought her was a mastmaker. He had purchased her to be a serving maid for his wife, but discovered upon returning home that all of his money and valuables had been stolen. Fatima, the man and his wife were forced to run the business by themselves. Fatima now learned the skill of making masts. Over time, the man granted Fatima her freedom, and she became his trusted helper.

One day he asked her to go to Java to sell masts for him. However, as she was sailing off the China coast, a typhoon struck and, once again, she was washed onto shore, far from home and penniless. She began walking inland, feeling confused and despondent over such bad luck. It so happens there was a legend in China that a female stranger would come from a far away land and make a tent for the emperor. There was great excitement about this event, because no one in China knew how to make tents. Each year, successive emperors had sent heralds out into the land requesting that all foreigners be sent to the imperial court.

When Fatima stumbled into a town, she was told she would have to report to the emperor. Upon arriving at court, the emperor asked her if she was capable of making a tent. She told him she thought she was capable. She made the rope from flax using the skills she learned from her father, the cloth was woven using the skills she acquired from the family of clothmakers, and the tent poles were constructed implementing the skills learned from the mastmaker in Istanbul. Putting together all of her knowledge, she was successful in constructing a tent for the emperor.

The emperor was delighted and offered to fulfill any of her wishes. She chose to remain in China. Eventually she married a handsome prince and was happily surrounded by children until the end of her life.

Of course, most of our lives will not be filled with change, challenge and chaos as dramatic as Fatima's. The Sufi story makes an important point, however, as it illustrates that each successive event of change/challenge/chaos leads to new and greater possibilities. It also shows that by cultivating the attributes of commitment and courage, we are capable of transcending life's challenges. Commitment to the quality of our lives instills a sense of certainty of our worthiness and is an effective mechanism for successfully obtaining our hearts' desires. Courage is companion to commitment as it provides the means to stay involved and engaged in the pursuit of our objectives. Commitment and courage pave the way for change.

Change, challenge and chaos are *exterior* events in our lives. They do not denote the truth of our inner core. The effects of change, challenge and chaos often feel as if a hurricane has struck, leaving havoc in its wake. In the middle of every hurricane is a center of calm, peace and balance. This center of calm has been referred to as the "eye of the storm" and exists simultaneously with outer chaos. It is advantageous to remember that there is a calm, peaceful place within us comparable to the eye of the storm. This is the core of our true nature which quietly awaits us. Fulfillment comes as a result of living in this quiet, calm, yet powerful center of our being.

Is there a Road to Fulfillment?

Dismiss whatever insults your soul.

Walt Whitman

Our society today is looking for a fast, easy, effortless road to fulfillment and contentment. We have not found such a road. Our travels can prove to be challenging, strenuous, and bumpy at times as we take risks and expand our awareness of ourselves and the world. At other times it is an exhilarating experience! It is the journey of life. We each choose which directions to take, how fast or slow we travel, and whether we will continue on a given route. Ultimately, the quality of our journey is of our own making. Our overall experience can be one of continual resistance perpetuated by fear and doubt, or an experience of trust and positive anticipation founded on love and acceptance.

Our lives' journeys often bring us to crossroads where we must choose directions. Let us choose the way which honors our true essence and nourishes our souls. Our only responsibility is to choose those paths which fulfill our hearts. Along life's highways there will be courses that hold greater interest than others, directions that hold more appeal, paths that possess a feeling of "rightness." Trust in our intuition will guide us to the path which leads to fulfillment. Why would we settle for less?

We all share the common desire to live in the state of happiness and fulfillment, our true nature. Fulfillment is a subjective condition based on an individual's belief system. What is appealing to me may be the next person's source of distress. The journey of life is a state of continual change.

This is normal and unavoidable. We offer these concepts as a vehicle through which you may gain insights and techniques to expand your choices, thereby living a richer and more fulfilled life.

OUR ONLY RESPONSIBILITY IS TO CHOOSE THOSE PATHS WHICH FULFILL THE DESIRES OF OUR HEARTS.

BE AT PEACE

FOR YOU ARE GREATLY LOVED

2

TRUST AND DOUBT

*You have to leave
the city of your comfort
and go into the wilderness
of your intuition.
What you'll discover
will be wonderful.
What you'll discover
will be yourself.*

Alan Alda

Leaving the Comfort of the Known: A Test in Trust and Doubt

Any time we undertake new journeys in life, we experience feelings of excitement in anticipation of the adventure we are about to begin. In contrast to the pleasant feelings of antici-pation, a sense of doubt may cast its shadow upon our enthu-siasm. Conflicting feelings of trust and doubt frequently ap-pear hand in hand as we venture into life's journeys, particu-larly the inward journey of the exploration of self.

Trust is the certainty which enables us to explore the many avenues of life and is a prerequisite for forward movement.

Possessing trust means "I'm capable," "I have a positive ex-pectation of life." *Doubt*, on the other hand, is the anchor which weighs us down and holds us back. Doubt is a belief that "I'm not capable," "I fear I'm inadequate." As we explore the dynamics of leaving the comfort zone, establishing pow-erful beliefs, and choosing to be accountable, we are afforded the opportunity of laying a foundation for trust and dispelling the seeds of doubt.

Apprehensive feelings often appear as we leave the com-fort of what is known and travel into unfamiliar, unknown ter-ritories. Taking this step requires trust as many doubts and fears may assail us. Remember the maps of the old world? There were charted territories that were the "known" world and uncharted territories that were the "unknown" world. Many old world maps held this dire warning of the uncharted terri-tory: "Beyond this place there be dragons." The new world would never have been discovered if all explorers had taken heed of that fateful warning.

Man cannot discover new oceans until he has courage to lose sight of the shore.

Anonymous

We often hear it said that we all fear the unknown. It is our belief that we do not fear venturing into the unknown as much as we fear leaving the safety and the comfort of what is known. The emphasis of *Journey Into Wholeness* is to move beyond the known in the form of self-imposed restrictions and limita-tions and into the unknown, uncharted realms which hold un-limited potential for a fulfilling and masterful life.

It is natural to want to be comfortable and secure in life; however, there is a price we pay whenever we choose comfort and limitation over forward movement and expansion. The price we pay begins with disquieting sensations of doubt, including: feeling stuck, trapped, stifled, bored, unfulfilled, powerless and resentful. We experience a lack of passion and zest in living. Remaining in the zone of familiarity is the consummate ticket to a life of boredom, stagnation and entropy. Some people call this zone of comfort the "self-worth zone".

The self-worth zone refers to an unconscious decision that each of us makes regarding the quantity we allow ourselves of any given commodity. We have a comfort zone or self-worth zone about every element in our lives: the amount of money we think we deserve; the quality and quantity of love we allow ourselves; how much happiness, joy, fun and peace we experience; the level of success we attain, or how excited and adventurous we allow ourselves to be. Whenever we find ourselves above or below this zone of comfort (self-worth), we experience *discomfort* and unconsciously take the actions necessary to bring ourselves back to the more familiar zone.

Comfort zones are built-in mechanisms within all of us. The question is not, "Do I have one?" but rather "How can I become aware of my self-limitations and move beyond them to my full potential?" True fulfillment in life tends to reside above and beyond the confines of the comfort zone. Until we possess the trust to step outside of our self-imposed limitations, it is unlikely that we will discover the many treasures that await us.

Venturing forth into the unknown regions within ourselves requires risks be taken. Perhaps the most challenging risk requires us to trust the certainty of our inner knowing and to recognize that the desires of our hearts hold purpose. Stepping out of our familiar zone of comfort takes commitment to ourselves and an honoring of our dreams. Having the courage to break out of the safety and familiarity of the known in life exposes us to the uncertainties of the unknown.

As we look back over our own lives, it has been easier to doubt ourselves and remain in the comfort and safety of our knowns rather than risk venturing into the unfamiliar. In our pasts we made choices to avoid risk and to remain in unfulfilling jobs and relationships much longer than was healthy. The pull for the safety and comfort of the familiar was stronger than the need to take care of ourselves. We allowed doubt to take precedence over trust.

REMAINING IN THE COMFORT AND SAFETY OF OUR KNOWNS ALLOWS US TO AVOID TAKING RISKS TOWARD THE FULFILLMENT OF OUR DREAMS. THE PRICE WE PAY IS A SLOW EATING AWAY OF OUR LIFE FORCE.

For us, the scales were tipped in favor of change (leaving the known) when the pain of remaining in unfulfilling jobs and relationships became greater than the comfort of familiarity we had so highly valued. Pain and discomfort are often the motivations that prompt many of us to leave what is known and open ourselves to change. Just as the fetus leaves the comfort of the mother's womb at the time of birth, we too must leave the comfort of our knowns in order to birth the next level of experience in our lives.

The desire to be safe and comfortable is innate within each one of us. The yearning for safety and comfort are basic human survival mechanisms that support life, and we all require periods of rest and relaxation between energy expenditures. Problems arise when we start to outgrow our comfort zones and refuse to leave their confines. The fetus must leave the womb at the time of birth because it has outgrown its place of comfort and remaining in the womb would result in death. Trusting our capabilities allows us to expand our comfort zones and grow and change. As we trust, we live and grow. To the degree we doubt, we remain static and die—emotionally, spiritually and physically.

It is impossible to experience the fullness of life unless we explore the unknown. The unknown holds the wonder, the mystery and the magic in life. Unexplored new worlds wait to be discovered and experienced. Unprecedented possibilities and opportunities present themselves in our lives when we are willing to step into the unknown.

Within the human heart lives a hunger, a passion, and an absolute certainty that life holds the potential for much more: more happiness, more joy, more love, more abundance, more fulfillment, more peace—MORE ! ! This journey supports you to venture forth out of self-imposed limitations and into the satisfaction that comes from expanding into your wholeness.

ULTIMATELY, ALL WE REALLY WANT IS WHOLENESS.

How do we define wholeness? What does it mean to be whole? The root words of wholeness are: health, holy, hallowed. Living in wholeness means that we are expressing the fullness and completeness of our true nature.

Accountability Supports Us in Our Journey

Accountability indicates that we have played a part in creating the circumstances in our lives: not just part of them, not just the ones that we are proud of, but *all* of the circumstances in our lives. As we recognize how we shape every element of our lives, we are truly powerful. Choosing to be accountable enables us to initiate steps toward changing life's undesirable circumstances by focusing on solutions to our dilemmas. Accountability is founded upon the certainty and trust that we are able to create what we want in life. One of the most important keys to self-empowerment is accountability.

WE ARE THE ULTIMATE ORCHESTRATORS OF ALL EVENTS IN OUR LIVES.

It feels as if we have nothing to do with the outcome of life's events. As a matter of fact, it often seems as if we are simply innocent bystanders to life's unfolding dramas. Every day the media are full of stories about the victims of incidents that occur throughout the world. There are starving children, survivors of natural disasters, the homeless, the abused, the sick and the suffering. These people certainly did not plan these destinies for themselves! Perhaps you find yourself questioning circumstances in your own life as you read these words, wondering about a car accident you had, an illness you are fighting, financial challenges you have suffered or problems in your relationships. You may be thinking to yourself, "Don't tell me that I 'orchestrated' all of this for myself! I'm not crazy!"

It would be ridiculous to suggest that any of us consciously plan life's challenges and misfortunes. However, we are multi-faceted beings with many levels of awareness. On deeper, unconscious levels, we draw to us every single occurrence in our lives, both positive and negative. Acknowledging that we are the ultimate orchestrators of all events in our own lives is called *accountability*. Choosing to be accountable for our experiences in life is an expression of trust which prepares and supports us for our journey into wholeness.

Accountability is a difficult concept to embrace because it is often confused with who or what is at fault. It is acceptable in our society to place blame upon ourselves or others for all that has been painful and disappointing in our lives. Many of us use blame to excuse things that are amiss in our lives: "He/she/it did it to me," "It was his/her fault," "It was an accident." Blaming others, the world, or ourselves, perpetuates victimhood. We become the victims of who or what we blame. Any time we find ourselves operating under the presumption that accountability is a matter of finding fault, we have lost our personal effectiveness. We become a victim stuck in the mire of a world of our own doubt.

Living as a victim implies we are powerless in our own lives and that the world and others control us. By assuming the victim posture we doubt ourselves and conclude we are ineffective and helpless. A belief in one's powerlessness sets us up for being a victim of life's circumstances. Victimhood is comparable to a cork bobbing in the ocean, helplessly at the mercy of the wind, weather and currents, with no guiding force of its own.

Accountability does not mean that we or others have failed. It has nothing to do with blame. We have not done something wrong. We are not being punished when we are faced with illness, relationship challenges, unpaid bills, unemployment, an accident, and so on. We are accountable—not wrong or bad or a failure.

ACCOUNTABILITY IS NOT ABOUT WHAT IS WRONG.
ACCOUNTABILITY IS ABOUT RETAINING OUR POWER.

Accountability supplies the point of power which surfaces through the conscious awareness: "I had something to do with creating the circumstance I am experiencing in my life. I choose whether to act as a victim, focusing on fault and blame, or to respond with awareness and take responsibility for my actions (be accountable)." As we create solutions to our challenges, we become highly effective—accountable.

When we choose to be accountable, we reclaim our innate strength. We unleash the power that comes with trust which lives at the core of our being and we denounce victimhood. In choosing accountability, we acknowledge that ultimately we shape our own circumstances. As we actively create the current circumstances with which we are contending, we may also actively influence different outcomes. We possess the necessary resources to reshape life's outcomes according to our will. We make lemonade from life's lemons rather than succumbing to difficulties. Accountability assists us to move up and out of our self-imposed comfort zones into new realms of possibility. We become masters (proactive), not robots (reactive), of life.

DOUBT KEEPS US POWERLESS, HELPLESS, HOPELESS AND STUCK IN VICTIMHOOD. TRUST IS A CHOICE WE MAKE THAT EMPOWERS US TO BE ACCOUNTABLE AND MORE EFFECTIVE IN LIFE.

Every circumstance in our lives offers the opportunity for gaining powerful insights which can propel us toward new levels of understanding. When we choose to be accountable for all that we experience, we are open to receive these gifts of awareness. Victimhood keeps us shrouded in unawareness. The quality of our lives is influenced by what we do with these presentations as we receive them. Ultimately, we create our own experience of life on earth, as either a heaven of trust or a hell of doubt, based on our personal belief system.

Our BELIEFS Perpetuate Our Experiences of Heaven or Hell on Earth

Every one of us began forming our unique set of beliefs even while we inhabited our mothers' wombs. We determined our sense of worth and lovability based on our perceptions as we were born into the world. We decided whether or not the world was a friendly place to live, adopted the spoken and unspoken attitudes of our parents and of the people around us and formed assumptions about how the world works and the parts we play in it. As we move through life, we continue to add to our collection of beliefs concerning everyone and everything we encounter, including ourselves. For many of us, most of these beliefs live at an unconscious level.

Our beliefs affect every single aspect of our experiences. When we have a good day or a bad day, a fulfilling job or a boring job, trusting attitudes or doubting attitudes, these experiences are filtered through our unique set of beliefs. These beliefs color every aspect of our world. Naturally, we like to be right about our beliefs. Nothing is more satisfying for many of us than being right: "I told you so," "I knew that relationship would/wouldn't work out," "I knew it would turn out this way." It is part of the human condition to enjoy being right, even if it is to our detriment!

It is as if we each wear a special pair of glasses, *belief glasses*, that selectively filter into our awareness evidence that supports an already existing belief. These imaginary belief glasses turn dark, photo-gray in order to filter out of our awareness any evidence that is contrary to a particular belief. We filter in what makes us right and filter out information that makes us wrong about any given belief. This is the function of selective awareness.

For example, many people in our world hold a firm belief about the terrible state of our planet, that mankind is on the brink of self-destruction. These people consciously and un-consciously fail to perceive evidence that suggests there is much positive change underway on our planet and that man-kind is evolving to a new level of cooperation. If we were to listen in on a conversation with a few of these people, we would probably hear: "The world is going to hell in a hand basket," "What is this world coming to anyway?" Their pri-mary focus in life is to look for pieces of information that support their belief in the demise of our planet. Other people believe that mankind is on the threshold of an advanced level of evolution. Their belief glasses filter out most of the mes-sages of gloom and doom and allow into their awareness the uplifting evidence that supports a better world: "Who would have imagined during the Cold War that the Berlin Wall would be taken down?" "People are making positive changes in our world." We allow into our awareness only pieces of proof that validate our beliefs—selective awareness.

OUR BELIEF GLASSES ALLOW INTO OUR AWARENESS
ONLY PROOF WHICH VALIDATES OUR BELIEFS AND
FILTER OUT EVIDENCE TO THE CONTRARY.

You may be wondering, "So what's the big deal about beliefs? We all have them." Yes, we all have beliefs. Prob-lems arise in our lives any time we are operating with beliefs that work against us. Beliefs which play on our doubts, such as: "I'm not lovable," "All men/women are impossible to live with," "Other people are _____ (fill-in the blank—smarter, better, more attractive, and so on) than I" tend to be self-fulfilling prophecies. We make ourselves right about any and all of our beliefs and *the universe cooperates.*

Fortunately, we can change our beliefs—they are not cast in stone. The key to changing our beliefs lies in identifying them for what they are and consistently being aware of how they influence the outcomes in our lives. Beliefs are a frequently untapped resource that are available to everyone. They hold unlimited potential for creating more of what we want in life. Trust in ourselves and our capabilities enables us to release restricting beliefs; we transform life's hells into heavens. (Doubt and fear keep us stuck in our limitations.) Beliefs are that powerful—*we* are that powerful.

OUR BELIEFS DETERMINE THE QUALITY OF OUR LIVES. BELIEFS ARE A POWERFUL, CREATIVE FORCE.

We all possess beliefs of which we are well aware: "I believe/don't believe in marriage," "I believe/don't believe in life after death," "I believe/don't believe we should eat dessert first." The above examples have an impact in our lives to the degree we personally involve ourselves in them.

The beliefs we are not aware of and have not examined are most often the ones that create difficulty. Many of our conscious and unconscious beliefs are built upon trust and assist us; conversely, many of our beliefs are based on doubt and work against us. When there are patterns and repeated circumstances that challenge us, we can look to our detrimental beliefs as the source of the difficulty. In the throes of recurrent challenging situations, you may have asked yourself, "Why am I doing this again?" or, "Why does this keep happening to me?" Of course, we want to retain the beliefs that strengthen us and release the ones that do not support us.

Maybe you are thinking, "Okay, so my beliefs are powerful. How do I know if I have beliefs I want to keep or beliefs I want to change? How do I get in touch with my beliefs?" The way to ascertain whether a belief is working on our behalf or against us is to look at the outcomes in our lives. The results we experience provide an effective resource to determine whether we are operating from a supportive or nonsupportive belief system. We invite you to look at some of the major areas of your life regarding the levels of satisfaction you are currently experiencing. How would you rate each of the following areas on a scale of 1 - 4, with 1 being the lowest satisfaction rating and 4 being the highest? Please take a moment to rate the following areas.

SATISFACTION SELF-RATING

Rating of 4 — Always satisfying
Rating of 3 — Usually satisfying
Rating of 2 — Sometimes satisfying
Rating of 1 — Never satisfying

My Job   _____
My Intimate Relationships   _____
My Spirituality   _____
My Health/Well-Being   _____
My Finances   _____
My Relationship with Myself   _____
My Life Over-all   _____

Ratings of 3 - 4 suggest that your beliefs are extremely supportive in these areas of your life, that you likely operate from affirming beliefs established in trust. Some examples of beliefs which would support a 3 - 4 outcome are: "I deserve to be happy, successful and fulfilled in my life," " I create what I want," "I am capable," "I am lovable."

If you rated any of the above areas with a satisfaction level of 2, this is an indication that there are some affirmative beliefs at work in those areas of your life. You undoubtedly are operating with beliefs that sometimes support you in having fulfilling experiences in these categories. Here are some examples: "I want to experience greater ____ (abundance, love, success, health.....)," "I am in the process of creating more ____ ."

With a 1 rating chances are good that your conscious and / or unconscious beliefs based on doubt inhibit your experiences of life in these and other areas. Unfulfilling experiences reflect the presence of limiting beliefs at work: "If only I ___ (had his/ her good looks, could get that promotion, could find Mr./Ms. Right, pay my bills...)." "If onlys" convey a belief in our own powerlessness. We feel victimized by our circumstances.

IF WE HAD NO LIMITING BELIEFS, WE WOULD BE LIVING FULLY IN THE EXPERIENCE OF OUR GREATEST DESIRES AND GOALS.

We Create Our Experience of Reality Through Our Beliefs

Our belief glasses (selective awareness) are an aspect of our unconscious minds. Their function is to make us right about our conscious and unconscious beliefs. The beliefs under which we operate become our truths and provide the foundation for what we experience in life. Through the universal laws of attraction, the beliefs we focus upon become our reality.

We live in a neutral universe where energy, such as a repetitive thought, attracts a parallel experience. Wherever we focus our attention, given time, that focus is provided for us through the laws of energetic attraction. If we believe in scarcity, our doubts take over and the unconscious will direct us to those circumstances which reflect our belief in not having our wants and needs met. Conversely, if we believe in abundance, trust leads our unconscious to attract to us those circumstances which uphold the belief in our wants and needs being met. The universe, through our conscious and unconscious minds, provides for us whatever we think about and believe in, both positive and negative. If we focus on what we want, that is what we will create. If we focus upon what we fear, what we fear will be experienced.

WHAT WE FOCUS UPON BECOMES OUR REALITY.

Our beliefs affect physical matter. Every belief and resulting thought and feeling we experience creates a chemical and energetic response within our bodies. We are mind/body energy systems who live and move in a world of energy. Energy is magnetic and neutral. Our beliefs and feelings create energy that draws to us whatever we put our attention upon. If I am preoccupied with the fear of not being able to pay my bills, I may soon find that I am experiencing challenges in paying my bills. If I am passionately excited about the new car I have been wanting, then I will find ways to create what I need to obtain the new car! The neutral nature of our world provides for us that with which we are preoccupied.

We can tell where our attention has been focused in our lives by the outcomes we experience: Am I living in a pleasant and supportive setting? Do I feel spiritually alive? Am I fulfilled in my career? Am I in good health? Do I feel I make a difference in the world?

BE CONSCIOUS OF WHAT YOU FOCUS UPON, FOR OUR
BELIEFS BECOME SELF-FULFILLING PROPHECIES.

The Power of Beliefs

In our culture it has been assumed that to realize a certain end result we must change what we *do*. In other words, the focal point for change has been on changing our behavior. For example, when people want to lose weight, they usually go on a diet and start an exercise program in order to change their bodies. Research has shown that in the case of dieting, the results are temporary. Ninety-five to ninety-eight percent of all dieters regain the weight they have lost—plus some extra weight! Any time we resort to behavioral changes alone we can count on short-lived outcomes, just as the overwhelming majority of dieters has experienced.

The difficulty with using behavioral changes in and of themselves is that changing behavior does not access our true source of power. Changing behavior is like changing the sheets on our beds or the clothing on our bodies. The efforts are short-lived, and pretty soon we feel that we will have to change them again and then again. Changing behavior is an attempt to change from the outside in. True and lasting power comes when we change from the inside out by shifting our beliefs.

ONLY BY SHIFTING OUR INHIBITING BELIEFS TO
BENEFICIAL ONES, (WORKING FROM THE INSIDE OUT)
CAN WE COUNT ON LONG-LASTING AND
POSITIVE OUTCOMES.

If you are not experiencing satisfaction in meaningful areas of your life, there are methods that can be used to shift the underlying beliefs and thereby set the stage for allowing more of what you want, shifting doubt to trust. Remember, our beliefs are extremely powerful tools for manifestation. When our beliefs are in harmony with our objectives, positive outcomes are certain.

Morgan: An Example of How Beliefs Work

Let us use Morgan as an example of the power of beliefs. Morgan is a fictitious character who, for our purposes, represents many people. As a child, Morgan was often invisible to his parents. His mother worked full-time, ran the household duties and attended to the needs of the other three children in his family. Morgan's father was frequently away on business. When he did spend time at home, he was preoccupied with catching up on household chores such as mowing the lawn and doing needed household repairs. In his spare time, he would sit in front of the television, go out for a game of poker, or golf with the guys rather than spend time with the kids.

As a result, Morgan was left in the care of many different people. He often played alone and began to doubt his own lovability and self-worth. It seemed no one wanted to take time for him because he was unwanted by, and an inconvenience to, the important people in his life. The only sure way he could count on having their undivided focus was to create trouble and suffer the consequences through being disciplined.

Morgan's belief glasses filtered in evidence which confirmed he was not important enough to receive love and not deserving or worthy of life's goodness. They filtered out any evidence to the contrary that indicated he was indeed lovable and worthy of happiness. His adolescent years produced distressing experiences which only strengthened his sense of unworthiness. In time, Morgan was convinced of the validity of his unconscious, self-limiting beliefs. Morgan's life was about living within the confines of a constricting comfort zone that compromised life's potential.

As an adult, Morgan found himself in a continual pattern of temporary relationships with women. Each woman he became involved with found reasons and excuses to end her relationship with him. This pattern reinforced his low self-esteem. He told himself, "I have rotten luck with women," "Bachelorhood is the only way for me," "I can't trust women." His deeper, unconscious beliefs were even more troublesome: "I don't deserve to be loved," "I'm not worthy of happiness," "I'm not good enough."

Inevitably, Morgan's experiences confirmed his collection of beliefs about himself. The universal laws of attraction drew him to women and circumstances which upheld his preconceived beliefs.

There is hope for all of the Morgans in the world, who hold inhibiting beliefs about themselves. Our beliefs can be transformed from self-fulfilling prophecies to tools of empowerment. This is where courage is required to step out of what is known and into the realm of unlimited potentialities. It may be tempting to close this book now and say to yourself, "I don't have the time to deal with this," "This is dumb," "Maybe I'll come back and do this exercise later." But perhaps some of you are excited and saying, "Great—let's get going!", "I'm ready, how do we begin?" Whatever you are experiencing right now regarding the exploration of your beliefs is appropriate. We en-

courage you to move at your own pace and be patient
with yourself.

Changing Beliefs

Becoming consciously aware of a detrimental belief is often
all that is necessary to release that belief and allow a life-en-
hancing one to take its place. The change process may be as
simple as saying to yourself, "I'm ready to let go of this belief.
This is what is true for me now...." When we become consciously
aware of our ineffectual beliefs, we are in a place of power. We
can now choose to change what no longer serves us.

Let us use Morgan's detrimental beliefs as an example of
changing beliefs. His internal dialogue may sound like this: "I
have believed that I have rotten luck with women. I have proved
myself right by setting up my relationships so they fail.

"I have been telling myself and the world bachelorhood is the
only way for me. I have been motivated by the fear that I may
never find someone with whom to share a committed relationship. I am changing what I believe. I know it is possible for me to
have a lasting and fulfilling relationship.

"I have believed I can't trust women. When I look back over
many of my relationships with women, I see this just isn't true.
There have been many women I have taken into my confidence
and befriended. I know in my heart that it is myself I have not
trusted, not women. I am adopting a new attitude—I trust myself, and therefore, I can trust others."

With the above changes in Morgan's beliefs, it is possible for
him to have different outcomes regarding relationships in his
life. In changing beliefs about relationships, he changed many of

his doubting core beliefs, such as: "I don't deserve to be loved," "I'm not worthy of happiness," "I'm not good enough." As is evident with Morgan's examples, even slightly changing one belief has a tremendous affect upon other related beliefs. These small changes build a trusting core and positively affect the overall quality of our lives!

CHANGING EVEN ONE BELIEF SLIGHTLY GREATLY ENHANCES THE OVERALL EXPERIENCE OF OUR LIVES!

It is imperative that a supportive, revised belief replace the eliminated one. "Nature abhors a vacuum" is as relevant to changing beliefs as anywhere in the system of our universe. Be conscious about what belief you use to replace the relinquished belief. Without conscious thought, it would be easy to replace a belief with another equally damaging one. It is necessary to adopt a new belief that will assist you in creating the experiences in life you desire.

The following exercise is not about doing, it is about being. It supports you in being effective in life.

SHIFTING BELIEFS EXERCISE

Step One

Select an area of focus.
Referring to your "Satisfaction Self-Rating" results, select one area in your life where you would like to experience greater satisfaction. (Examples: career, relationships, love, sexuality, spirituality, self-esteem, health, intimacy.)

Step Two

Determine your current belief.
We evaluate whether a belief is working for or against us by considering the results in our lives. When we are dissatisfied

with the outcomes in any given area of life, we want to ask ourselves, "What do I believe about myself regarding my contribution to the current outcome?" Continue asking this question of yourself until you find a belief that resonates within you. Truth is a *felt* experience—pay attention to your body. It will let you know when you have touched upon what is true about your beliefs. The following examples suggest bodily sensations which may indicate a truthful belief: flutters in your stomach, a flushed feeling, ringing in your ears, sweaty palms, increased heart rate, or chills.

Step Three

Examine the belief.

Imagine that you can step outside yourself and objectively explore this belief. Use your logic as well as your feelings to become intimately familiar with this belief and the power you have given it. Take time to concentrate upon the effect it has had in your life. Be as objective as possible. This step is about becoming familiar with an element that has had an impact in your life, not about making yourself wrong—or right.

Step Four

Make a conscious choice to relinquish the belief... or to perpetuate it.

After you become deeply familiar with your belief, it is time to choose whether to accept it or release it. Both choices are valid. The point of power comes from being consciously aware of the beliefs that determine the quality of your life. This step assists you in moving from a reactionary, powerless mode to a proactive one.

Step Five

Replace the belief with an "upgraded" one.

When you choose to relinquish your belief, it is important to replace it with a belief that will support you in realizing the results you want. We are not talking about using positive affirmations that feel like we are lying to ourselves. The goal here is the next level of truth that we can embrace. Remember Morgan's adopted beliefs. He replaced his initial beliefs by using statements such as: " I deserve...," "It is possible for me to...." With time, Morgan can raise his current belief to a higher truth that embraces greater potential.

Step Six

Remain conscious of your upgraded belief until it is fully integrated.

Do whatever it takes to keep the newly upgraded belief in the forefront of your awareness. Some people take a few moments each day to meditate upon their newly adopted belief. To reinforce this new way of thinking, place a written copy of the belief where you frequently see it. Say the belief to yourself in order to assist in its integration. Create a collage or piece of art that symbolizes the special meaning of your belief. This can be an inspiring way to remain aware of its special implications for you. Have fun with this step! Trust yourself to know what actions support this new belief in becoming more vital and alive.

BY SHIFTING OUR LIMITING BELIEFS AND ADOPTING NEW ONES, WE OPEN OURSELVES TO UNLIMITED POSSIBILITIES. THE TRUE SOURCE OF CREATION BEGINS AND ENDS WITH OUR BELIEFS.

As you fully integrate the new belief, you may choose to focus on another area of life in which you would like to experience greater satisfaction as well. This exercise can be utilized as often as you like. It is most effective to complete one area of satisfaction before moving into another area of focus.

Remember, this is a life-long process for most of us. There is no need to rush to the finish line—none exists!

BE AT PEACE

FOR YOU ARE GREATLY LOVED

3

LOVE AND FEAR

Fear is like a great fog. It sits on your brain and blocks everything—real feelings, true happiness, real joy. They can't get through that fog. But you lift it—and buddy, you're in for the ride of your life.

Mr. Bob Diamond, *Defending Your Life*

There are but Two Motivators in Life— Love and Fear

At the deepest level of every feeling in the world lives either love or fear. At any given time we are stimulated by one or the other of these primal feelings. Many schools of thought have suggested there is ultimately only one core feeling and that is love. Behind every fear-based feeling lies a yearning for acceptance, for a sense of connection, and for the reassurance we matter to ourselves and each other.

Love is acceptance. When we are motivated by love, we are accepting of our life experiences. The experiences can be pleasant, wonderful and positive, or they can be challenging, hard and negative. The key factor in determining whether we are motivated by love or fear is whether or not we are open and receptive to life's experiences.

Fear is resistance. Any time we find ourselves denying, avoiding or escaping our experiences, fear is the motivator. We are capable of not only resisting the negatives, but we can be equally effective in resisting the positives. For example, let us say that I am ecstatically delighted about my new romance and that I want to shout my love and happiness from the roof tops! But I have bought into my social conditioning which places limits on how happy and expressive I can be at any given time. Instead of allowing myself to shout from the roof tops I squelch my enthusiasm. When I speak to others about my love relationship, I remember what I have been telling myself: "This may not last and I had better 'be cool'...." I deny myself the authenticity of my feelings of joy and excitement and instead adopt a doubting, fear-based attitude. I give fear (resistance) more power in my life than love (acceptance). Invalidation of my experience places me in limitation and fear.

LOVE IS ACCEPTANCE. FEAR IS RESISTANCE.

As a whole, our society fears (resists) expressing and allowing our true feelings. Fear has run rampant as the primary motivator. The realm of feelings has been frightening ground upon which to tread.   How many of you grew up hearing phrases like "Don't be.... sad, angry, hurt, afraid," "Be a good girl/boy," "Act like a man/adult," "Big boys/girls don't cry." The underlying message is: Do not act in alignment with how you really feel. Allowing and expressing our true feelings has been a social taboo for eons.

Social "niceties," historically, have prevailed over authenticity. We learned at some point in our lives that in order to be loved and accepted and to receive approval, we must not show emotions considered to be unacceptable, uncomfortable, disturbing or upsetting to another. Greater value is placed on being nice than living in our truth. Only socially acceptable emotions are allowed expression. It is as if we are at war within ourselves trying to keep our true feelings hidden and not let them be seen, for the risk is too great. With time, it becomes easier and easier to become estranged from our feelings. This alienation process seems normal in a world where authentic feelings are not condoned.

The Avoidance of Feelings

There are many "methods" available to avoid feelings. One often relied upon method for the avoidance of feelings is to "go to our heads." Our intellect takes over when we go to our heads, making it easier, safer and less confrontational for ourselves and others. Feelings and emotions are the domain of the heart, the feeling center. By going to our heads, we escape the discomfort, inconvenience and vulnerability of allowing our feelings to be expressed. Instead, we change our focus to figuring it out, or making sense of our feeling experiences. The analytical, thinking, left brain approach is highly prized in our Western culture. Trusting and relying on our feelings and inner knowing (right brain activities) is often considered a shortcoming, an ineffective female trait that lacks "good sense."

Another method that is widely used in our society to avoid feelings is the reliance upon compulsions and addictions. Our compulsions and addictions serve a purpose; they set the stage for a shift in our emotional states. All of us want to feel good and have pleasant emotional experiences. Our compulsions and addictions are the "tools" we use to temporarily avoid unpleasant feelings. Many of us overwork, overexercise, undereat or overeat, overspend, drink alcohol, take drugs, become television couch potatoes, spend long hours at the computer or become involved in addictive relationships. All of these compulsive patterns share a common thread. They refocus our thoughts and actions into our compulsion(s) rather than confront the genuine experience of our underlying feelings.

We pay high prices for denying, avoiding and resisting our feelings. We pay with our physical and emotional health, with elevated levels of stress, and with an erosion of our own self-trust and self-respect. By resisting our feelings and emotions, we deny, avoid and resist the truth of our uniqueness. In this resistance, our life force becomes depleted.

Feelings and Emotions

In order to share a common language, let us differentiate between "feelings" and "emotions." Feelings are a consciousness or an awareness that registers in our bodies. (That is why they are called feel-ings.) They are the *unexpressed* predecessors to emotions. Feelings provide the foundation and motivation for emotions.

Emotions are responses to feelings. Emotions are feeling-energy in motion. Perhaps you have heard the common definition of e-motion: "e-nergy in motion." Emotions are the expressions, responses or reactions to our feelings. Feelings can be transformed to emotions either by outward expression or inner experience.

A FEELING IS AN UNEXPRESSED BODILY AWARENESS.
AN EMOTION IS A RESPONSE TO A FEELING.

Some examples of feelings are sadness, happiness, anger and excitement. If we do not fully experience or express a feeling (awareness that resides in our bodies), it remains a feeling. If, on the other hand, we choose to allow and/or express a feeling, it then becomes an emotion.

- The e-motion for sadness may be the outward expression of crying. The inner e-motion experience of sadness may be fully allowing myself to feel loss or grief.

- The e-motion for happiness may be the outward expression of laughing. The inner e-motion experience of happiness may be allowing my inner joy.

- The outer e-motion for anger may be to voice my dissatisfaction aloud. The inner e-motion experience of anger may be accepting and validating what I am feeling.

FEELINGS BECOME EMOTIONS WHEN WE FULLY EXPERIENCE THEM INTERNALLY AND/OR EXTERNALLY.

The Greatest Stumbling Block to Allowing Feelings

There has been an emphasis in the human potential movement the past several years to uncover our feelings and allow them expression. Science and medicine have come to the conclusion that expressing our feelings is beneficial to our health. So why do we not just go ahead and allow ourselves to feel what we feel and healthfully express those feelings? After all, if we allow ourselves to feel, to experience fully what is going on inside ourselves, it can be over and done in a matter of moments. Why the fear about feelings? What is the resistance about?

THE REASON WE DO NOT EASILY ALLOW OUR FEELINGS IS THAT WE BELIEVE WE MUST CHANGE THEM OR MAKE THEM BETTER.

When we make an automatic assumption that we have to right a wrong feeling, we feel overwhelmed. Is there any one of us who can effectively eliminate our feelings or fix them and make them better? Would life be easier if we could simply avoid feelings?

Our True Nature—An Ocean of Feelings

An expansive ocean of feelings resides in the depths of our beings—active, alive and unfathomably deep. Feelings come to the surface of our consciousness as do waves of the ocean, in continual motion, ebbing and flowing with the rhythm that is life. Our only "job" is to allow the waves of feeling to come and go. Attempting to resist the ongoing sea of feelings is akin to resisting nature itself.

What a relief—not to try to change, fix or make our feelings better! By accepting and allowing all aspects of our feeling nature, the feeling energy moves freely through our body's energy systems. When this feeling energy is allowed clear passage, we are open to live in the fullness of life's experiences.

OUR ONLY OBLIGATION IN THE REALM OF FEELINGS IS TO ALLOW THEM.

Resistance to Feelings

We create havoc for ourselves any time we attempt to resist and block the natural flow of feeling energy. Feelings such as anger, sadness, doubt, envy and loneliness, as well as happiness, pride, excitement, beauty and sensuality can be equally open to resistance. We would like to pick and choose only those feelings we judge as good or acceptable and keep out the bad or unacceptable.

Feelings are neutral. They are neither bad nor good—they simply are. An ocean is not good or bad; it exists as part of nature. Anything, including feelings, becomes good or bad only if we judge it so. Concluding that certain feelings are positive and others negative sets us up for continual struggle with promoting the good and avoiding the bad.

FEELINGS ARE NEUTRAL ENERGY—NEITHER BAD
NOR GOOD.

By allowing the entire spectrum of feelings, we experience the richness and fullness of life. Try as we might, it is impossible to pick and choose specific feelings. We either embrace our feelings, or we resist them. In other words, we approach our feelings in an accepting, love-based manner or a fear-based, resisting one. Our life's energy can be completely exhausted in the struggle that results from resisting feelings. In that struggle we are left with few, if any, resources for fulfillment.

Each of us has a comfort zone concerning the quality and quantity of feelings we allow into our awareness and experience. Some of us thrive on situations that promote stress, and stress becomes comfortable for us. Others allow only so much intimacy, love, peace and joy. Remember, we each form our own zone of comfort around every single element in our lives, and feelings are no exception.

When we expend energy into stifling "bad" feelings, we also stifle the "good" ones. We cannot have one without the other. Many of us have found methods to stifle our feeling experiences in order to remain in our particular zone of comfort. However, our experience of life will look similar to the flat-line reading on a heart monitor machine when the heart stops functioning—flat and dead. We are surviving, and that is about all there is to say about the quality of life. There are less hurt feelings and ups and downs in life, also an absence of joy and fulfillment. There may be no anger, yet there are health challenges. Grief and sadness may not be felt, and neither will the opportunity to heal the circumstances which created them. Life is flat, dull and futile when we remain in avoidance of feelings.

The Purpose of Feelings

In order to experience genuine happiness, we must allow ourselves to experience sadness. We cannot know one polarity without the other. To know love, we must be aware of what we fear. To know joy, we must have had experience with despair. And to know trust, we must know doubt. Each expression balances and breathes life into the other. Wholeness comes with being willing to experience all of our feelings, knowing each one has a purpose in our lives.

Because those who do not know how to weep do not know how to laugh either.

Golda Meir

We experience fright for purposeful good. Fright assists us to be aware of a potential threat and allows us to make conscious choices about our well-being. When we experience grief, it, too, possesses a beneficial purpose. Grief allows us to mourn the loss of someone or something meaningful in our lives and it promotes healing. Without the expression of grief, it would be impossible to move beyond loss. Anger serves a powerful purpose. When the circumstances in our lives are out of alignment and our needs or expectations are not being met, anger lets us know. Experiencing anger makes possible the correction of conditions which have created our distress.

Every feeling has significance. Feelings serve as the bridge between our inner world and the outer world.

Choosing Responses to Feelings

One of life's certainties is that we all have feelings. Our only choice is how we respond to them. We can either allow our feelings or resist them. We do not fear experiencing feelings as much as we fear how we will react to them. This fear stifles the recognition that feelings are neutral. Feelings are as much a part of our world as are the incessant waves of the ocean. Freedom comes with trusting that our responses to feelings need not be harmful to ourselves or others.

Maybe you have harbored the fear that if you begin to allow your feelings, there will be no end to them—you will cry buckets if you remove the stopper from your sadness and hurt or harm someone or something if you unleash your store-house of anger. The thought of expressing the depths of your love may be the emotional equivalent of exposing yourself to hurt and vulnerability. Any fears that arise at the thought of expressing feelings are normal, healthy responses to raising our levels of comfort in the world of emotions. When we contemplate stepping up and out of our self-imposed limitations, fear often raises its head. That is its job—to keep us safe within the confines of our comfort zones.

Feelings Do Not Die

Feelings are a special type of energy. A challenging aspect of feeling energy is that it does not disappear or die simply because it has been resisted, denied or avoided. Feeling energy has a life of its own. Because we cannot see this energy or feel it does not mean that it disappears into thin air. We cannot effectively terminate this energy, try as we might; it cannot be destroyed—only changed or altered. When wood burns it appears to be consumed and destroyed by fire. It is not destroyed, however, its energy simply has changed form to become smoke and gases. Similarly, the energy of feelings can be changed, but not eliminated.

Resistance to feelings stays with us as "stuck energy." Energy is movement and action. It must be allowed free motion in order for it to evolve. The stuck energy of suppressed feelings will eventually find a way to move. These thwarted feelings sit like a magnet in our unconscious and attract more and more like-energy. With time this conglomerate of energy will rise and give conscious expression to itself.

This energy dynamic often expresses itself in a manner that can prove to be challenging to ourselves and others. For example, we may have let our unexpressed anger build up inside of us until one day something as mundane as spilled milk proves to be the match that sets off the molten volcano of wrath seething beneath the surface. Rage takes over and leaves a trail of damage in its wake. Resisting feelings can create challenges in other areas of life: financial challenges, challenges in our relationships, mental, emotional or physical challenges. We may experience a pervasive sense of futility and depression that clouds our lives. Or we become numb and move with lethargy through our days.

Science has produced conclusive evidence that disease is greatly influenced by how we deal with our feelings. We are a mind/body system. Our thoughts and feelings create a chemical reaction within our bodies, and when our feelings are stifled, this stuck energy often appears as a disease or physical illness. When we allow free movement of our feelings, regardless of their nature, our physical bodies become healthier. The onset of physical illness or disease is perhaps one of the most debilitating risks we take when we resist our feelings.

Maybe you find yourself curious about giving your feelings greater expression. Perhaps all you have known and experienced in the realm of feelings are the two extremes of suppression or reaction. How does one go about responding to feelings in a healthy way?

The Middle Road

There is a way to allow and express our feelings that is healthy and life-giving. We call it "The Middle Road." The Middle Road is a safe, effective and sane way of honoring and allowing expression of our feeling nature. It is a choice that has validity, and it works. We will share with you how to utilize this method for yourself. First, let us explore the other two options.

Option One: Suppression and Projection

Suppression is the act of stifling our feelings. When feelings are suppressed, we temporarily keep our experiences of them locked away in our unconscious. There the energy of the feeling remains in latent form, building upon itself.

When we suppress our feelings, we deny the truth of our inner reality. There are numerous ways to suppress feelings. We suppress our feelings by denying them, talking ourselves out of them, making them wrong or relying on our compulsions. Suppressing feelings is the equivalent of trying to hold an inflated beach ball under water. It takes a tremendous amount of life's energy to control what naturally wants to move up and out. We can hold the beach ball of our feelings down for a while, but eventually something must give, and when it comes popping up into conscious awareness in our lives it can create quite a splash!

As we suppress our feelings, we become numb to other feelings. Suppression requires more and more of our effort with time, and this squelches our enthusiasm for life. We no longer find joy in waking each day, and we may find ourselves being irritable and cranky with life's inconveniences. A sense of powerlessness and distress result when our feelings are restrained.

Projection occurs when we place our unowned aspects onto others. These projected aspects can be positive as well as negative; however, most often they are negative. When I am projecting negatively, it appears that the other person is guilty of what I perceive to be his/her shortcomings. It looks perfectly obvious that the other person caused my experience, and I feel justified in pointing the finger of blame in their direction. I can even call on others to join me in my projections and they will agree with me.

What we fail to conceive in the state of projection is that the "outside" person or circumstance reflects our unresolved feelings. Others are mirrors of ourselves. We can only perceive in others what lives in us or what has the potential to live in us. So when we admire a quality in another, we are relating to a quality that resides in us or lies latent within us. Negative reactions to another is the response to the aspects of ourselves that we find worthy of judgment. Projection is the act of assigning responsibility to another for our unrecognized experiences.

Suppression, as was mentioned earlier, is a temporary attempt to keep our feelings at bay. Eventually the suppressed energy will build and make itself known in our lives. Through projection we transfer our unconscious issues onto another. Projection effectively allows us to cut ourselves off from the aspects of ourselves which we do not want to claim. Suppression and projection create a state of imbalance and inner turmoil which makes it exceedingly difficult to express our innate whole and complete nature.

Choosing the road of suppression and projection will eventually lead to a dead end.

Option Two: Reaction

Reaction is the act of transferring the focus away from fully experiencing a feeling. This is accomplished by acting upon the feeling rather than opening fully to the feeling experience. Like suppression, reaction is fear-based and lacks self-empowerment. It is as if we respond like robots—press a button, watch the robot react. Press another button, the robot reacts again in a different manner. Resolution of a feeling is not possible in the state of reaction. As a matter of fact, reaction to a feeling causes it to be more deeply ingrained within us. Reaction is frequently the outcome of suppression.

When we react to a feeling, it often appears to be a powerful release. It may look as though I am really getting my anger out by throwing the china against the wall. I could even be telling myself: "I'm really letting go of my anger!" When I have broken my last piece of china, I may even feel a sense of relief, at first.   Then, with time, I notice that there is a growing and pervasive sense of uneasiness, a feeling that there is something off, and I am not able to put my finger on it. I have given my power away to my feeling and allowed myself to be provoked by it. I have acted upon rather than accepted my feeling completely.

In reacting to our challenging feelings, we are attempting to relieve ourselves of the tension that accompanies such feelings. Acting on the feeling is a transference of energy, not a release of energy. With reaction, the feeling itself is denied, resulting in the reinforcement of stuck energy.

We are not suggesting that you control, resist or limit your feelings because that would be suppression. The key element to address with reaction and suppression is: "Am I responding to my feelings with an attitude of allowance and love, or am I resisting my feelings out of fear?" The underlying motivator with both options of suppression and reaction is fear. Fear promotes contraction, a virtual shutting down of our life force and its available energy.

Option Three: The Middle Road

The Middle Road is beautiful in its simplicity. It is the act of allowing direct experience of feelings. It is neither suppression nor reaction. It lies between these two options. When we choose The Middle Road, we allow ourselves to move into our feelings. We acknowledge that what we are experiencing is enough and we do not try to change, deny or react to how we feel. We accept the feeling, integrate it, and move on with our lives. The Middle Road is motivated by love.

In choosing The Middle Road, we are claiming our true power. Only by honoring and allowing our feelings are we in a place of strength. We no longer expend our energy in resistance and we have ample reserves to create a life that is satisfying and complete. This is not to suggest that we do not have *preferences* for what we would like to experience. The Middle Road is not complacency. We no longer struggle to stifle the energy of the natural ebb and flow of our life, the innate ongoing nature of feelings.

To allow The Middle Road expression, it is necessary to be open rather than closed to our experiences. This requires us to take some degree of risk and step up and out of our zone of comfort into the realm of feelings. We accomplish this by believing that allowing expression of feelings is more important than suppressing and reacting to them.

In choosing to allow the depth of our feelings, love and acceptance become our motivation rather than fear. With love as our motivator, we open ourselves to unlimited expansiveness, growth and to the full potential of ourselves as humans. Our life force is more available for expressing our wholeness and the creation of fulfillment.

To feel what we feel, we must allow our experiences to fully occupy our conscious awareness. In accepting and allowing our feeling nature, we find that feelings can come and go freely in a matter of moments. It is only in the resistance to feelings that we experience the phenomenon of pain. (More on that in Chapters Four and Six.) When we allow our feelings, their fluid energy advances naturally, the way it is intended. We do not have to act on feelings to resolve them.

There may be times when we have a tendency to outwardly express some of our feelings. We find ourselves laughing when we experience happiness or joy, crying tears of grief or sorrow, or jumping up and down in a state of excitement and enthusiasm. The above examples are responses, *not reactions* to feelings. There is a difference. In responding to feelings, we allow them to move with the natural flow of their expression. The road of suppression cuts us off from our feeling experiences. With reaction we are in resistance to feeling. We go into the robot mode which finds relief from the internal tension we feel by redirecting our focus elsewhere through an outward expenditure of energy.

By allowing ourselves to be consciously aware of what we feel, and accepting what we feel, the dynamic is set in motion for releasing that particular feeling. *It is that simple.*

FULLY EXPERIENCING OUR FEELINGS ALLOWS
THEIR RELEASE.

Feeling Our Feelings Makes Healthy Boundaries Possible

One of the gifts of being consciously aware of feelings is that they provide a resource for creating a sense of safety and well-being in our lives. As was mentioned earlier, all of our feelings possess purpose and meaning. The feelings of anger, dread and fear can act as red flags, warning us of potential harm, danger, inequities and imbalances. When we experience a sense of ease, joy and deep contentment, these feelings, too, represent the state of our personal world. Feelings are the vehicles for inner communications that indicate the conditions of our inner and outer lives.

When we experience an upsetting feeling such as anger, dread or fear, we can choose how we will respond. We can dismiss and suppress the uncomfortable feeling, react to it by diverting our energies elsewhere, or respond appropriately to it by trusting its validity.

Here is an example. Let us say that I am a (female) secretary for a high-powered (male) executive. A deep sense of uneasiness has escalated within me over the past few months in regard to my boss. I have not taken the time to fully explore my feelings, I just know I feel uncomfortable with him. His occasional invitations for coffee have turned into a daily routine. During these coffee breaks together, he reveals details of his personal life to me—details I would rather not be privy to. He is a good conversationalist, always picks up the coffee tab, and is a gentleman. ("Why am I so uncomfortable? He's only being friendly.") I try to push my uneasiness to the back of my mind when he looks at me a little too intently given the professional relationship I think we share.

The feelings of discomfort turn to panic and anger when he asks *me* to accompany him to our competitor's annual industry cocktail party. He has a wife at home he could have invited! I begin to doubt myself and I wonder, "Have I encouraged him to think that there is a personal nature to our relationship? Have

I acted in a way that he considers enticing by accepting his coffee invitations? What am I going to do about this? I'm afraid I'll lose my well-paying job!"

This fictitious dilemma would not have taken place had my boss and I been setting and maintaining healthy boundaries. Had there been the presence of healthy boundaries, I would not have accepted my boss' daily invitations to coffee, and he would not have asked. If healthy boundaries were present, my boss would not have confided deeply personal information, and I would not have allowed it. Had healthy boundaries been in place, my boss would not have invited me to the party. I would not be concerned about losing my job with my refusal to accompany him. If I had a clear sense of my boundaries, I would not be doubting myself about my relationship with my boss.

HEALTHY BOUNDARIES CREATE HEALTHY
RELATIONSHIPS.

What Are BOUNDARIES?

Boundaries are invisible lines that separate where our personal space ends and another person's begins. They help us feel safe and define our true sense of self and what we are about in the world. The only true parameter of setting and maintaining healthy boundaries is how we feel. When we do not allow our feelings, it is impossible to set and maintain healthy boundaries.

Quite often when we feel discomfort in the presence of another person, our boundaries are being violated in some way. When we feel safety and comfort in the presence of another, this means our boundaries are likely being respected. It is up to each one of us to set and maintain healthy boundaries.

Our boundaries typically change with the circumstances in our lives and the people we encounter. In the love and safety of an intimate friend or partner, our boundaries are smaller and more inclusive in order to allow the quality of connection we desire. With a person that we perceive as a threat, our boundaries may expand so enormously that it would be challenging to find their perimeters. Establishing flexible boundaries gives us the ability to experience what we want and keep out what we do not want.

HEALTHY BOUNDARIES LET IN WHAT WE WANT AND KEEP OUT WHAT WE DO NOT WANT.

There are two basic categories of boundaries: physical and emotional.

(1) Physical boundaries. Our physical boundaries include our bodies and our physical possessions. We determine our physical boundaries by choosing if, when, where and in what manner we allow another to make physical contact with our bodies or our belongings. Any time another person makes physical contact without our agreement, it is considered a physical boundary violation.

Examples of physical boundary violations:

- Someone borrows something of mine without my permission.

- I receive unwanted sexual advances.

- Someone steps on my foot, spills something on me, bumps into me.

- My car or home is broken into.

- My personal possessions are lost, stolen or damaged.

- Another person enters my bathroom, bedroom or other private area without my consent.

- Physical abuse is directed toward me.

We set and maintain our physical boundaries by being clear within ourselves where our personal boundaries begin and end. We determine our boundaries by *how we feel*. These boundaries will likely change with the people and circumstances in our lives. We expand our personal boundaries with some people, and with others we contract them. It is ultimately up to us as individuals to create our own safety by determining the parameters of our physical boundaries.

(2) Emotional boundaries. Our emotional boundaries give definition to who we are. They represent what feels safe and appropriate. They protect our unique set of ideas, beliefs, feelings, values and how we look at the world. Emotional boundaries are determined by how we allow others to treat us. They encompass the manner in which another addresses us, what words or expressions are used in a given communication, and whether there is respect for our individuality, our specific needs, values and desires.

Examples of emotional boundary violations:

- Someone attempts to convince me to think, believe or act the way they want.

- I am criticized for my personal outlook, values, beliefs or opinions.

- I am involved in a relationship where I or my partner compromise our individuality to be okay with each other.

- Someone slanders me or directs abusive language towards me.

- I am ignored or neglected by a significant other.

- My personal desires and needs are not treated with respect.

OUR EMOTIONAL HEALTH IS DIRECTLY RELATED TO THE HEALTH OF OUR BOUNDARIES.

It is interesting to note that any time there is a physical boundary violation, an emotional boundary violation automatically accompanies it. If you will refer again to the list of physical boundary violation examples, you will notice that in every circumstance an emotional response accompanies the physical violation. The emotional response likely takes the form of anger, fear, frustration, hurt or resentment. These emotional responses act as warnings to indicate a boundary violation has taken place.

WHENEVER THERE IS A PHYSICAL BOUNDARY VIOLATION, AN EMOTIONAL BOUNDARY VIOLATION AUTOMATICALLY ACCOMPANIES IT.

Regardless of the *intention* of the boundary violation, whether it was purposeful or accidental, it is still a boundary violation and will require setting parameters that are acceptable to you. When we mentally excuse someone's boundary intrusion by telling ourselves: "I'm sure they didn't mean it,"

"It was an accident," "They didn't do it on purpose," we send ourselves the message that we have to endure the boundary violation and that another person's needs and wants come before our own. We become powerless victims of ourselves and others.

Without healthy boundaries we are prone to the influences of others. Our experience of life is one of ineffectiveness, powerlessness and helplessness. Without effective boundaries in place we set ourselves up to be the victims of others in our world, or we victimize others through lack of boundary awareness. Establishing healthy boundaries is pivotal to staying out of victimhood and reclaiming our personal power.

We are not suggesting that you become aggressive or offensive to others in creating healthy boundaries. Honor yourself in a manner that feels right for you by sending the message that you value yourself and expect to be valued as well. Setting and maintaining healthy boundaries is a two-way function. When we are certain about our own boundary management, it becomes natural for us to respect the boundaries of others as well.

Healthy Boundaries Raise Us to New Levels of Effectiveness

As we grew into adulthood, many of us had no healthy role models for setting and maintaining boundaries. If you came from a dysfunctional family, chances are extremely high that you were not supported in creating healthy personal boundaries. One of the elements that makes a family dysfunctional is the lack of healthy boundaries. You may have been told that you do not have the right to assert limits. With the conditioning many of us have experienced concerning boundaries, we can expect to need improvement in establishing a stronger sense of self-identity, self-respect, self-trust and self-love.

By setting and maintaining healthy boundaries, we are empowered to be highly effective. As we strengthen our physical and emotional boundaries, we create a deeper sense of who we are and what we choose to experience in life. Clarity about ourselves defines our relationships with others. We project a message to ourselves and to the world: "I am worthwhile, my wants and needs matter, I have respect for myself and I expect others to respect me as well." It starts with us. When we raise the standards of what we allow into our lives, others are inclined to respond with increased respect for our boundaries as well. With some people, however, we may have to actively defend our boundaries.

Often the most challenging aspects of setting and maintaining healthy boundaries, is giving ourselves *permission* to do so. It is as if there is a voice of fear in the back of our heads asking, "Who do you think you are?" "How dare you!" "You are going to alienate people!" (More about this voice of fear later.) If you find yourself contending with internal fear-based messages, you can choose to step out of self-imposed limitations (comfort zone) and into the freedom of new territory. The presence of the fear-based, critical voice is an indication that change is about to occur. Building healthy physical and emotional boundaries is a choice of personal empowerment based on self-love.

SAYING "NO" TO WHAT WE DO NOT WANT AND "YES" TO WHAT WE DO WANT IS THE PRIMARY WAY TO CREATE HEALTHY BOUNDARIES.

Unhealthy Boundaries

Our discussion has centered so far on healthy boundaries. To have an understanding of healthy boundaries, it is helpful to know the elements of unhealthy boundaries. Boundaries become unhealthy due to issues of (1) proximity or (2) their specific nature.

Unhealthy Proximity Boundaries

A boundary qualifies as unhealthy when a person's personal boundary is either too close or too far away in relation to the significant person involved.

Let us take the example of a fictitious couple, John and Anne. If they distance themselves physically or emotionally from one another, their intimacy level dissipates. If on the other hand, John and Anne's boundaries overlap so closely that one of their boundaries is on top of the other, these unhealthy boundaries contribute to an accompanying loss of individuality. They will find themselves lost in each other with no clear definition of where one individual begins and the other ends. This type of unhealthy boundary is called "enmeshment." Eventually the "consumed" person will feel overwhelmed, suffocated and stifled in the relationship. Enmeshment, like distancing, contributes to relationship failure.

Unhealthy proximity boundaries can impact all types of personal encounters and relationships.

Examples of physical and emotional distancing boundary violations:

- My significant partner closes down emotionally and ceases to share information of an intimate nature with me.

- I am four months pregnant, and I have not yet shared this information with my husband.

- My brother is angry with me and refuses to see me or speak to me for an extended period of time.

- A close friend has moved without leaving a new address.

- My date spends the entire evening at the party talking and joking with friends. I am left on my own with people I do not know.

- I am a department store clerk who is chatting with a co-worker while ringing up customers' sales. I am so involved with my private conversation I ignore the customers.

- My friend invites a person I do not know to have dinner with us. Rather than opening the conversation to common areas of interest, I choose to exclude the new person by introducing topics that relate only to my friend and myself.

Overlapping boundaries tend to occur most frequently when there is a long-term, co-dependent type of relationship. Significant partnerships, family members, parents and children, work relationships and close friendships can be vulnerable to overlapping boundary violations. The long-term result of overlapping boundaries is resentment culminating in overt or covert rebellion by the person feeling violated.

Examples of overlapping boundary violations:

- My partner speaks for me, or I speak for my partner: "We want to do this," "You don't want to do that."

- My partner makes decisions for me or makes choices that affect me without my input. Or, I make choices for my partner: "We're going to Disneyland for our vacation," "I selected what you are going to wear today," "I invested all of our retirement fund into a venture capital company."

- I participate regularly in an activity I dislike in order to please my partner.

- I feel a need to ask my partner's permission before proceeding with even small matters, such as having lunch with a friend.

Overlapping boundaries are the equivalent of being devoured by another person without thought of personal preferences. The devoured person becomes selfless. It is a situation that is ripe for the dynamics that create victimhood. Healthy intimate relationship boundaries allow both partners to maintain their individuality while being in their relationship. There is room to breathe and to grow while interacting with one another.

Nature of unhealthy boundaries

The specific nature of unhealthy boundaries is either one of being too rigid or overly flexible. Both extremes create challenges to attaining a high quality of life.

The *too rigid* person has a boundary that resembles a brick wall. The wall is thick, high, inflexible and impenetrable. The world is very black and white, making change or growth threats to security. This creates an extremely lonely and isolated life.

Rigid people do not allow others to get close to them; therefore, life becomes narrow, very limited and routine.

The other extreme is the *overly flexible* boundary holder. An overly flexible person's boundary resembles a broken, twisted rubber band. They attempt to mold and shape themselves to be what others expect them to be and take on the views, opinions, beliefs, attitudes and feelings of others. They lack a true sense of self and allow anything and everything to enter their life experience. As a result, the overly flexible person often feels overwhelmed, out of control and confused. This person is a perfect candidate for being manipulated, abused and neglected by others.

Establishing Healthy Boundaries

When we possess healthy *emotional* boundaries, all other kinds of boundaries are easily established and maintained. We establish healthy emotional boundaries by creating clarity about our personal preferences. As mentioned earlier, giving ourselves permission is necessary for establishing healthy boundaries. The following exercise is a declaration of your emotional boundaries.

MY PERSONAL RIGHTS

The following are examples of personal rights. Please write your own ongoing list of personal rights. Remember, you are the ultimate authority as to the appropriateness of all boundaries you establish and maintain.

I have the right to...

- make my wants and needs at least as important as any one else's.
- feel my feelings.
- ignore the advice or criticism of others.
- tell my truth.
- protect my privacy.
- my own beliefs.
- change my mind.
- live my life exactly as I choose.
- say "no" to what I don't want.
- say "yes" to what I do want.

Start your list with ten personal rights and continue to add to your list as you encounter additional dislikes and preferences.

Creating healthy boundaries consists of:

1) Consciously living my personal rights.
2) Telling the truth to myself and others.
3) Being aware of my feelings and honoring them, regardless of their nature.
4) Expanding the knowledge of my personal likes, dislikes, needs, wants, desires, passions and preferences.

The healthy boundary is like a fence with a gate that opens and shuts when needed. The gate opens to allow into our experience what we want. It opens when we say "yes." The gate shuts out what we don't want to allow into our experience. It closes when we say "no."

Our responsibility is to be clear about our yeses and our noes. With that clarity, we have the ability to set and maintain healthy boundaries.

BE AT PEACE

FOR YOU ARE GREATLY LOVED

4

ACCEPTANCE AND JUDGMENT

What we resist persists.

Anonymous

Acceptance and Judgment: Key to Transformation

Many of us are attracted to the deep inner transformation that is experienced as we explore the cultural and scenic wonders of our planet. These experiences dramatically alter how we view ourselves and our world. Our lives are no longer the same. We are entering territory on our journey into wholeness which holds the potential for similar inner transformation. Let us explore acceptance and judgment.

Love is acceptance of our life experiences, fear is the state of resistance and judgment. Moment by moment we choose which of these motivators will prevail. Our society (and our entire planet) has been operating on fear-based impulses for eons. Neighbor mistrusting neighbor, nation against nation, us against them. How will we will turn the tide of suspicion and fear?

We can all contribute to the overall well-being of our world by shifting our focus from fear to love, from resistance to acceptance. The power of love and acceptance is magnetic. Because we live in a neutral universe, the focus of our thoughts, feelings and attention determines what is drawn into our reality. We are masters of our universe and are capable of creating either a paradise or a world of disease, scarcity and destruction. The quality of life in our world originates within each one of us—our thoughts and actions affect the whole. We are accountable for our own well-being as well as that of the entire planet.

Compassion as a Personal Tool

An important contributor to personal and planetary evolvement is the capacity to be compassionate. Compassion is acceptance and love *in action*. It comes from the heart and goes beyond sympathy and caring. It is the ability to permit empathy and tolerance for ourselves and others rather then finding fault. Compassion allows us to accept "what is" and shift our focus from resistance to taking the actions necessary for resolution. For example, rather than simply hoping for world peace, we initiate peace within ourselves which radiates out into the world. Compassion breeds honor, dignity and respect.

On a personal level compassion provides a mechanism which gently and effectively supports deep, inner exploration. When we are challenged by self-doubt, we take compassionate action by acknowledging the doubt and conducting an inner investigation to reveal the path to self-trust. This is compassion in action. Compassion is acceptance of all feelings, thoughts and experiences enabling us to take the actions necessary to take care of ourselves and others.

Lasting change occurs in an atmosphere of safety. The acceptance which comes from compassion establishes the safety we need to expand into our full potential. Criticism, as we will explore later in this chapter, is the antithesis of compassion. A partnership of love and criticism cannot exist. Love and acceptance in action (compassion) open the gate to change while criticism of self and others locks the gate tight. Compassion provides a key to unlocking the gate of transformation.

Compassion in action exists when:

- I allow and accept my feelings of anger and frustration when my car breaks down. Acceptance of my feelings provides the means for me to reclaim my inner calm, enabling me to resolve my dilemma by calling for assistance.

- I allow and accept my feelings of grief when my beloved pet dies. I feel safe enough to honor the depth of my feelings by allowing myself the time it takes to release my tears and hold a simple, loving ceremony in remembrance of my pet.

- I accept and allow my feelings of inadequacy when I make a mistake. With acceptance I permit myself the opportunity to explore my fears rather than falling into my usual pattern of self-criticism.

COMPASSION IS LOVE IN ACTION.

Compassion for self allows compassion for others to be possible. To have a personal relationship with compassion, we must understand the dynamics of judgment. Judgment stands between us and the peace that compassion brings.

A Fresh Perspective About Judgment

Our social and religious conditioning has told us over and over again, "Don't judge," "A good person does not judge." In our efforts to be socially upstanding, we have tried not to judge. How many of us have succeeded in not being judgmental? How often have we reprimanded ourselves for making judgments thinking that eventually we will overcome them?

As an alternative to judging ourselves because we make judgments, we offer a different, unprecedented course of action. This approach to judgment will undoubtedly generate some controversy as it challenges some deeply- cherished and long-standing points of view.

Judgment can keep us stuck in fear and resistance. We move beyond judgment by allowing ourselves to have judgments. Yes, you read correctly—ALLOW THE JUDGMENTS. We know it sounds outrageous: "Allow myself to have judgments—don't make myself wrong for judging—having judgments is all right?" For some of you this may sound a little scary. To others this concept may sound like great fun! Still others may breathe a sigh of relief with the freedom that comes with telling the truth at last. Perhaps it is comforting to know that you are receiving an invitation to expand your comfort zone by altering your beliefs about judgment.

WE ALL MAKE JUDGMENTS. IT IS PART OF BEING HUMAN.

Judgment is a part of our human nature and provides the opportunity for self-exploration and learning. Conscious awareness of our judgments enables us to discern whether we are in a state of love and acceptance or in a state of fear or resistance. Being aware allows us to make choices that support us. Our effectiveness is not determined by whether we are in fear or love, but rather by our level of awareness. Awareness and acceptance allow us to progress from judgment to discernment in order to transform our experiences of life.

The following examples illustrate how awareness and acceptance transform judgment:

- Knowing that Johnny has been teased at school allows me to shift my judgment of his cranky behavior to compassion, give him a hug and support him to explore his feelings.

- Being aware that I overeat to cope with my feelings of self-doubt grants me the understanding and compassion to release my judgment, explore this feeling and get support.

Since we all make judgments, regardless of our attempts not to, maybe it is time to adopt a new way of looking at judgment. *Perhaps trying not to judge is simply setting ourselves up for one more thing to judge ourselves about!* Telling ourselves not to judge is the equivalent of telling ourselves not to breathe or eat or have sex.

Judgment versus Discernment

In our discussion about judgment, it is important to distinguish judgment from discernment. Discernment is a process which uses our reasoning, intuitive and feeling resources for making effective choices. It enables us to distinguish what fills our hearts with certainty and peace from what does not. It is achieved by accepting and respecting ourselves and others.

Discernment empowers us to have *preferences* for what we want without being critical of other options. Some of us prefer vanilla over chocolate, and others prefer chocolate over vanilla—one is not better or worse than the other. We may not approve of others' decisions or actions but our respect for others remains intact. We recognize our own and others' inner wholeness. Through discernment we effectively perceive options which serve our highest good and make decisions based on the clarity of these perceptions. Discernment perpetuates a state of inner peace, calm and certainty. Compassion allows discernment.

DISCERNMENT IS BASED ON LOVE AND ACCEPTANCE AND ENABLES US TO MAKE SELF-VALIDATING CHOICES.

Judgment, on the other hand, is a fear-based mechanism focused on defining good or bad, right or wrong, fault or blame. Our inner fears cause us to be judgmental rather than discerning.

The majority of us experienced invalidation and judgment throughout our formative years. By the time we reached adulthood, we were self-invalidating and self-judgmental. Self-judgment can take many forms, such as a sense of self-doubt or feelings of inadequacy. For many of us the pain of our self-judgment has become so great that we project it onto others through blame. When we blame, we step into the role of victim and give our power away to others. When we judge without moving to discernment, we become immobile and ineffective.

We determine when we are in the state of judgment or discernment by the feelings we experience. When we are unaware that we are judging ourselves or others, our judgments do not resolve or dissipate. Resentment escalates along with our increasing sense of self-righteousness regarding who and what we are judging. We become agitated and uptight. We are compelled to prove the other person wrong (and ourselves right). We point out how bad they are (and how good we are) and how justified we are in our blame (and how faultless we are). Good, bad, right, wrong, fault and blame are the focus of judgment. Internally, we feel ill at ease, distraught, angry, victimized and resentful when we judge others. Judgment is a state of nonacceptance based on resistance (fear). We resist the other person and their actions because we resist aspects of ourselves. Left unchecked, judgment is caustic and destructive to ourselves and others.

Annaliese's Story of Judgment and Discernment

The following story from Annaliese's personal experience presents an example of how judgment functions.

Annaliese and her husband, David, live on a semi-private lake in the woods of northern Idaho. It is a popular destination for friends from the city who want a respite from the noise, activity and hustle of urban life. On one occasion some visitors came for several days and, because of weather conditions, were confined to her home. With each passing day, Annaliese's resentment grew steadily towards one of the guests, causing her to be impatient and abrupt with this person.

Annaliese was disconcerted by her inner state and strong sense of judgment. In an effort to move through her judgment, she talked about her feelings with her husband and a close friend. Instead of diminishing, her judgment and resistance toward the visitor escalated during her conversation. Life was presenting an opportunity for learning and she resolved to get to the bottom of her experience.

She took time to meditate on her dilemma and discerned that her judgment of the visitor represented deeply buried fears within herself! Her guest was a living example of her own worst fears! Her guest reflected her fears about not honoring herself, not being able to produce change and not moving beyond self-limitations. She was clearly presented with the opportunity of bringing unconscious fears into the light of her awareness.

Compassion for herself came alive as she began to understand her hidden fears. Her awareness heightened and she was able to make conscious choices about her situation. As she developed compassion for herself, compassion for her visitor also developed. With compassion, she was able to shift from judgment to discernment.

UNDERSTANDING AND AWARENESS MAKE COMPASSION POSSIBLE. JUDGMENT EVOLVES TO DISCERNMENT THROUGH COMPASSION.

Since that time, Annaliese has chosen not to pursue her friendship with that guest. She has set her personal boundaries by not opening herself or her home to someone to whom she is not attracted. However, she is grateful for the learning opportunity this particular visit presented, for it allowed her to expand her awareness by transforming her darkness (the unknown) into light (knowledge). This was neither easy nor comfortable, but it proved to be enlightening!

A note about judgment: In our desire to prove ourselves right about our judgments, it is tempting to gather agreement about our point of view from those around us. It appears obvious to us (and others) that we are right and the "offender" is wrong. Of course, our righteousness strengthens our attachment to remaining in judgment.

Every Judgment Carries the Gift of Awareness

It is helpful to realize that we would not have judgments unless there were hidden and unresolved fears alive within us. Looking within, we recognize our deficiencies are mirrored to us by another. If we had no fears, we would not be judgmental.

OUR JUDGMENTS MIRROR OUR UNRESOLVED FEARS.

Every person and event in our lives has the potential to function as a mirror for us. If this were not so, we would not respond or react to others. The elements we commonly share with another (consciously or unconsciously) determine our emotional responses. Others reflect our inner strengths, as well as our inner fears of inadequacy.

MIRRORING EXERCISE

Here is a short exercise on mirroring: Think of a person who inspired you by their beauty, intelligence, humor or strength. This person served as a reflection of your innate beauty, power, intelligence or humor. If this attribute were not already present within you, at least potentially, it would be impossible to experience it in another. As you bring the other person's admirable quality to mind, acknowledge that you share this attribute. Focus on this realization for a few moments in order for it to fully register within you.

Now, think of a negative opinion you have formed of another person. Bring to mind the nature of your negative impression. Beneath the judgment is a commonly shared "inadequacy." The person you held in judgment simply reflected an aspect of yourself that you resisted. Take a moment to acknowledge the fear of inadequacy that this person has reflected for you. As you do so, commend yourself for having the courage to look within the shadows and bring a hidden aspect of fear to light. Understanding hidden fears is made possible by becoming aware of your resistance. Understanding elicits compassion and compassion allows discernment. A shift from judgment to discernment creates one of life's miracles—true peace.

Mirrors reflect positively and negatively. Our responsibility as individuals committed to wholeness is to have the courage to look into the mirrors.

Pain is a Result of Resistance

Now we are about to see how judgment enters the picture in relation to pain. If you find yourself yawning, holding your breath, getting bored or becoming agitated during this section, please understand that these are mechanisms we all use from time to time to defend our comfort zones. Take a break if need be. Our intention is that by the time we complete this discussion, you will be on your way to understanding the concepts concerning pain, resistance and judgment. Whether you accept them or not, of course, is up to you. These ideas may be considered by many to be radical and unusual. Allow yourself the time it takes to explore these previously unknown territories.

We all experience emotional and physical pain at one time or another. Pain is not a feeling, but rather the result of resisting our feelings and judgments. As discussed in the previous chapter, energy becomes blocked when feelings are not accepted and allowed. The feeling energy becomes stuck and accumulates in our bodies resulting in discomfort and pain. Feelings are benign message carriers from our inner world when we allow them expression.   Another way of expressing this idea is: judgment produces resistance; resistance creates pain. Our unallowed feelings and judgments are the source of pain.

Judgment > Resistance > Pain

In the case of physical pain, the same dynamics are at work. Physical pain is a result of bracing oneself against (resisting) a physical bodily sensation. When we experience pain, our tendency is to tense our muscles and hold our breaths. By relaxing into the pain with slow, deep breathing and loosening the muscles of the body, the uncomfortable sensation passes. When using relaxation techniques, pain becomes a different experience. Relaxation allows our brains to release pain-blocking chemicals called endorphins, the natural equivalent to prescription pain-relief drugs. Prescription pain killers block the pain receptors in our bodies so that pain is not felt. Our natural pain-relief system is allowed to become activated when we are able to *relax* into pain.

There has been extensive research in the area of physical pain in recent years. Dr. Jon Kabat-Zinn, nationally renowned author, scientist and teacher, has made a wonderful contribution to pain relief at his Stress Reduction Clinic. He recommends meditation, yoga and visual imaging to assist his patients who are experiencing chronic physical pain such as back pain and headaches. He has been extremely successful in his endeavors. His underlying premise is to move into the pain, rather than resist it. It appears the way to the other side of pain is to go through it.

PAIN IS THE CONSEQUENCE
OF RESISTANCE

(Authors' note: We acknowledge that there are many different types of pain, some of which require professional intervention including the use of pain killers. Our discussion here is focused on general emotional and physical pain.)

Accepting our thoughts and feelings of judgment allows us to become aware of the messages of fear contained within them. Compassion for ourselves and others develops as we gain understanding of the fears that lie hidden in our judgments. Compassion transforms the fear behind judgment into acceptance and discernment. When we allow our judgments to shift to discernment, we can effectively change the circumstances in our lives.

THE WAY THROUGH RESISTANCE AND THE RESULTING EXPERIENCE OF PAIN IS TO ALLOW JUDGMENT.

Acknowledge and Allow the Judgments

Resisting our judgments only serves to cement them firmly in place (what we resist persists). We would like to share a method for moving beyond judgment and fear into acceptance. This technique provides the tools necessary to become discerning.

EXERCISE: TECHNIQUE FOR
ALLOWING JUDGEMENT

Many people who use this technique refer to it as the "Triple A Technique": Acknowledgment and Allowance move us into Acceptance—(AAA)

Step One

Acknowledge the Judgment.

To accept judgment, we must possess awareness of it through conscious recognition. Feelings and beliefs that were unconscious are brought into our consciousness. One of the ways to accomplish this is to be observant of our judgments. As we notice them we can respond internally with an acknowledging statement such as "That was a judgment." Remember, this is not about making ourselves wrong for having judgments, but rather an exercise in cultivating awareness.

Step Two

Allow the feeling.

We recognize we are in judgment (rather than discernment) by our internal emotional state. Unallowed judgment produces agitation, self-righteousness, a be-right, make-wrong attitude and pervasive inner turmoil. Our tendency is to ignore, deny or suppress our feelings. By allowing our feelings we can move from resistance to acceptance and discernment. We accomplish this by acknowledging that it is all right to have our feelings. All feelings are valid, and when we experience them without attempting to change them, we develop understanding and compassion.

ALLOWING FEELINGS RELEASES THE JUDGMENT AND RESISTANCE THAT RESULT IN PAIN.

Step Three

Accept Accountability.

To allow judgment and become discerning, it is necessary to be accountable. As discussed in Chapter Two, accountability is acknowledging that we create our experiences. An example of being accountable is saying, "I may not like what I'm

experiencing right now; however, I hold myself able to produce a different outcome." Accountability is a tool which leads
us to live in an empowered state.

Using the above technique, we move out of resistance into
acceptance, from fear to love, from powerless to powerful,
from victims to directors in our lives. This technique is effective any time we are in a fear-based state and wish to transform our experience to that of acceptance and love. Using
this technique promotes an enhanced experience of life. It is
important to note, however, that we cannot force this shift
upon ourselves. Be gentle and patient.

When we are not in a state of self-acceptance, we become
victims of our fears. Anything that is not an expression of
acceptance and love becomes an expression of fear. To move
from fear to love, we acknowledge the truth of our experience. By acknowledging and allowing our feeling experiences,
we automatically move into acceptance and discernment. We
move from fear, resistance and judgment to acceptance
and love.

(1) Acknowledge the experience + (2) Allow the feelings =
(3) Acceptance (Love)

ALLOW MY
FEELINGS

LOVE

ACCEPTANCE

ACKNOWLEDGE
MY EXPERIENCE

FEAR

VICTIM

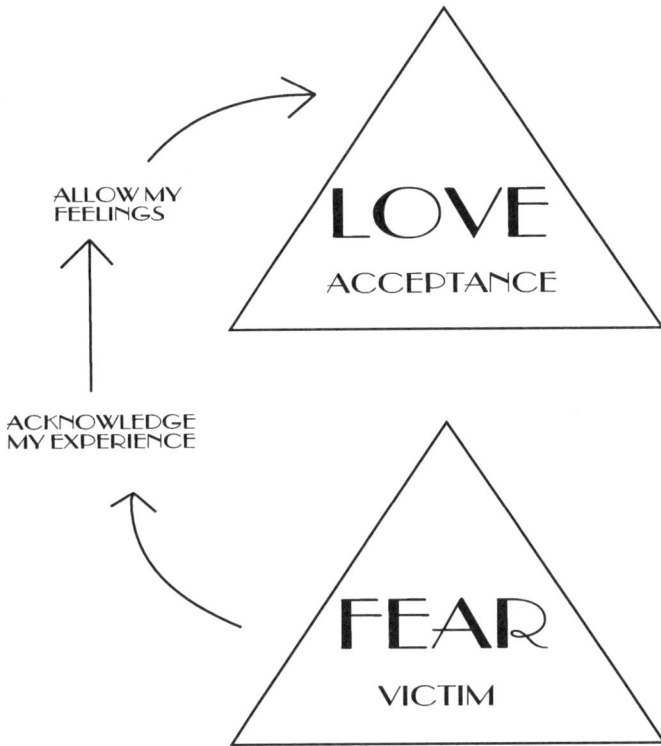

Faultfinding messages in our minds are a form of judgment that keep us stuck in fear and inhibit self-acceptance. These messages create an obstacle to living in compassion for ourselves. Our next area of focus will be upon internal negative self-talk: the "critical voice."

The Critical Voice

Conformity is the jailer of freedom and the enemy of growth.

John F. Kennedy

Have you noticed the presence of a judgmental, faultfinding "voice" that seems to come from inside of you? You know the one we are speaking of—the critical voice that says, "I look awful today," "I should have done this," "I shouldn't have done that." The role of the critical voice is to inform us of our many shortcomings.

What is the critical voice and how did we acquire it? The critical voice is the accumulation of all the negative, judgmental, authoritative messages we have recorded in our memory throughout our lifetimes. It is a conglomeration of internalized attitudes, opinions and beliefs we have adopted as our own from influential figures such as our parents, family members, friends and teachers. We have merged all of the authoritative messages together into a combined resource pool we call the critical voice. It is especially focused on social conformity. It operates from fear.

The critical voice is not an expression of our true nature. We have come to believe it is a part of us because it has permeated our awareness and its messages are convincing. We have either followed the advice of the critical voice or rebelled against it.

THE CRITICAL VOICE IS NOT OUR TRUE ESSENCE.

When we speak of the critical voice, we are not referring to the supportive and positive voice of the conscience: the loving, still voice within. The voice of the conscience is distinct and opposite in its form and function from the critical voice. It serves the invaluable function of instilling awareness within us so that we are enabled to make conscious choices and decisions that support our forward movement. The voice of the conscience is love-based and cultivates growth and self-expansion. The critical voice is fear-based and promotes conformity and self-limitation.

The critical voice is comparable to an automatic tape player that is activated under particular circumstances. The combined resource pool of authoritative messages broadcasts into the loudspeakers of our minds. The broadcast message from the critical voice is interpreted as self-criticism.

A primary focus of our authority figures is to help us conform to society's standards so we become socially acceptable people. The method for accomplishing this goal has been handed down from authority figure to authority figure through time. The proven method for teaching conformity has been the use of fear-based negative messages in the form of criticism. In the absence of our authority figures, the critical voice steps in to "motivate" us with self-criticism.

SELF-CRITICISM IS THE METHOD USED BY THE CRITICAL VOICE TO COMPEL US TO CONFORM.

Self-Criticism Promotes More Self-Criticism

There is a pervasive belief in our society that criticism leads to change. The belief suggests that if we are hard enough on ourselves (if we allow the critical voice full expression) we will be motivated to become more effective. Nothing is further from the truth. The outcome of self-criticism is simply more self-criticism.

Consider the following example: I am about to have an interview for a long-awaited career opportunity. I have struggled through many long years of higher education, gotten my degrees, and now the big moment is upon me—the job interview. What do you think my outcome will be if my self-talk prior to the interview goes like this: "I know, I'll never get this job. I have no experience. Besides I look like hell today. Maybe I just won't show up for the interview. Why bother?" Do you think I will make it to the interview, let alone be hired for the job? As this example illustrates, the critical voice can be debilitating when left to its own devices. It can render us completely ineffective. Yet many of us give credence to this combined pool of negativity and allow this voice to govern our every decision and action.

Allowing the critical voice to run rampant as a motivational tool is highly ineffective. Attempting to inspire ourselves before running a marathon by beating ourselves with a baseball bat is the equivalent of using the critical voice as a motivational tool. Instead of feeling strong, capable and ready to run, we will be trying to pick ourselves up to run a 26-mile race after having just abused ourselves to the point of powerlessness. The critical voice operates the same way on an emotional level, except it is much more subtle than a baseball bat. The results are the same—we are rendered powerless by giving credence to its caustic messages.

SELF-CRITICISM IS EXTREMELY INEFFECTIVE AS A MOTIVATIONAL TOOL.

If we allow the critical voice to run our lives, we remain within the fear-based confines of our comfort zones (self-worth zones) and do not venture beyond our self-imposed limitations where life holds excitement and promise.

Identifying the Critical Voice

The question may arise, how do we know when we are contending with the critical voice? The most effective method to recognize the presence of the critical voice is by assessing HOW WE FEEL. The critical voice operates in a negative, defeating way. The critical voice is in action when we doubt ourselves, feel powerless and ineffective, are judgmental, feel defeated, or have lost our self-trust, our self-assurance and our certainty. The critical voice is functioning any time we are tempted to give up and quit. The critical voice operates with speed and subtlety. The messages are perceived as "me talking to me." The critical voice has become so familiar to many of us that we don't even question it—we simply accept its messages as The Truth.

We all have a critical voice, a unique set of acquired negative messages. Who or what has power in our lives—the conglomerate of critical messages or us?

Rules of Operation of the Critical Voice

Rule #1
The critical voice DISTORTS REALITY. Its message is flawed because it twists a portion of reality. It is this distortion that causes distress in our lives. If you will notice, the voice uses extreme ideas. making any given situation appear at its absolute worst.

Rule #2
The critical voice is skilled in SPEED AND SUBTLETY. The messages sound reasonable and we readily assume their validity. The reasonableness of the critical voice is an effective hook for keeping us stuck in our limitations. It is insidious.

Rule #3

The voice perpetuates a SENSE OF POWERLESSNESS and being out of control. When we feel ineffectual, hopeless, helpless and weak, guess who is running our lives? Yes, the critical voice.

Rule #4

The critical voice is FEAR BASED. When we fall prey to our fears, the critical voice is in control. Destructive, negative, fear-based thoughts belong to the critical voice.

Mastering the Critical Voice

What do we do with this critical voice that influences our lives? The critical voice is like anything else in life that we desire to change. Attempting to overpower it, make it wrong, ignore it or talk back to it feeds it our power and energy and only serves to perpetuate it. To change the critical voice requires acknowledgment and respect rather than resistance. What we negate, we empower.

EXERCISE: STEPS TO CRITICAL VOICE MASTERY

First Step

Tune in to the critical voice. Notice when it is playing its adverse messages over the loudspeakers of our minds. We can tell the critical voice by its tone: it is judgmental, unkind, stern, authoritative, demeaning and controlling. Remember, the most trustworthy way to identify the voice is by how we feel. When we feel anxious, diminished, defeated, hopeless, helpless, depressed, guilty or resentful, the critical voice is in control.

Second Step

Acknowledge that its messages are no longer useful. Recognize that the messages of the critical voice are outdated. Identify the messages as adopted beliefs, opinions and criticisms of the authority figures in our lives. We have made these harmful messages our own. We can choose to release them and take back our power.

Third Step

Respond appropriately. We respond to the messages of the critical voice by taking a stand for ourselves which we accomplish by directing an inner dialogue asserting our truth. The critical voice sends its fear-based messages when we take risks, such as when we tell the truth about how we feel to our partner: "How inconsiderate and thoughtless you are! Look at poor ____ (your partner). He/she is devastated."

Our internal dialogue in response to the critical voice could sound something like this: "Hello, critical voice. I hear you. I know that you want me to be nice and not hurt people's feelings—AND—I am learning to speak my truth while respecting the feelings of others."

Addressing the critical voice is most effective when we acknowledge its messages and speak respectfully to it (in the same respectful manner we like to be addressed). Follow your acknowledgment with an "AND" and state your rebuttal in a straightforward, clear and nondefensive manner. *And* is used instead of *but* because but negates everything that was stated before it: "I know you have my best interest in mind, critical voice, *and* I am learning to trust myself," "I acknowledge I made a mistake, *and* I choose to be compassionate with myself." By mastering the critical voice, we reclaim personal power.

Winning and Failing

We have explored a few of the elements required to cultivate compassion and transform judgment into discernment. These concepts often do not come easily. Please have patience with yourself and know that as long as you stay involved in your learning process, you cannot fail. Failure only occurs when you give up—when you stop attempting to reach for your dreams and goals. You are winning as long as you keep on keeping on!

BE AT PEACE

FOR YOU ARE GREATLY LOVED

5

LIGHT AND SHADOW

*We are all two people, one daylight and one we keep
in darkness.*

Bruce Wayne a.k.a. Batman from *Batman Forever*

Light and Shadow Defined

The children's classic, *Beauty and the Beast*, illustrates an intriguing and often misunderstood polarity: light and shadow. The Beast represents (mirrors) the unacceptable, fear-producing aspects that live in the shadow (the unconscious). When Beauty initially encounters the Beast, his appearance frightens her. She asks him to move out of the darkness and "come into the light" to better perceive him. The Beast reveals to Beauty his deepest, darkest aspects including his anger, his fear and his vulnerability. As Beauty accepts the Beast just as he is and appreciates his inner beauty, magic happens! The Beast transforms into a handsome prince—the shadow becomes light!

In our culture we seek the light and avoid the dark. It is commonly accepted that only light is favorable and beneficial and that the shadow (dark) is to be feared and avoided—like the bogeyman in the closet. In this chapter we will explore the value of both light and shadow and recognize that each has a unique function and cannot exist without the other.

Light, for our purposes, is defined as "conscious aware-ness." We define the shadow as "unconsciousness or unaware-ness." Awareness of our anger grants us knowledge of its presence and resides in the light. When we are unaware and unconscious of the presence of our anger, it resides in the shadow. To illuminate the meaning of light and shadow, let us explore the function of these two opposites.

LIGHT IS AWARENESS / KNOWLEDGE. SHADOW IS THE
LACK OF AWARENESS / THE UNKNOWN.

Light: Home of Awareness

Light is the home to all conscious feelings regardless of the kind of feeling. Anger, sadness, grief, happiness, delight, terror, sorrow and joy, all feelings of which we are aware and in knowledge of, reside in the House of Light.

Shadow: Home of Unawareness

The shadow is the home of all unconscious, repressed, sup-pressed, denied, avoided and disallowed feelings. The feel-ings that live in the House of Shadow can be exactly the same as those that reside in the House of Light. It is a matter of awareness. Anger, sadness, grief, happiness, delight, terror, sorrow and joy can reside in the House of Shadow as well as the House of Light.

CONSCIOUS FEELINGS LIVE IN THE HOUSE OF LIGHT. UNCONSCIOUS AND REPRESSED FEELINGS LIVE IN THE HOUSE OF SHADOW.

Light and shadow exist within each other, and without each element we become unbalanced. These two opposite and complementary qualities are called yin and yang in Eastern traditions. Yin is feminine, receptive, negative, *dark* and small. Yang is masculine, active, positive, *light* and large. Everything in creation is a merging of these opposite qualities flowing in and out of one another. When we look to nature, we see that the brightest sunlit day casts the darkest shadows. A clear, dark night is lit by the moon and stars. In what appears to be dark, there is always light and in what appears to be light, there is always dark.

Yin/Yang

Have you had an occurrence in your life that was distressing at the time it happened, such as losing a job, ending a relationship, getting delayed in traffic, or having an important event canceled? Have you noticed that these and other outward misfortunes have often provided the opening for more rewarding experiences? In retrospect, you may have discovered that the loss of your job provided the impetus necessary to pursue the career you had only been dreaming about, or that the termination of your relationship created the space for your soul mate to step into your life. Perhaps being stuck in traffic prevented your involvement in a traffic accident further down the road, or an unexpected opportunity appeared where the anticipated event would have precluded its arrival.

Life is a combination of yin and yang, shadow and light, challenge and ease, night and day, male and female. Each element contains a portion of the other and complements and completes the other.

LIGHT AND SHADOW CANNOT EXIST WITHOUT THE OTHER. THEY ARE INTERDEPENDENT ELEMENTS. EACH ONE GIVES FORM, DEFINITION AND MEANING TO LIFE.

The Shadow: Source of Creativity

The shadow is often limited to mean only that which we fear and attempt to avoid. When the shadow is restricted to this definition, we miss the rich process which provides the opportunity for creativity. The shadow is the home of our unconscious mind and is the source of our creativity, which is diminished when it is denied. In allowing our formerly unknown feelings, we possess the potential to move beyond what has been blocking us and create what we want in life. Our goal is not to rid ourselves of the shadow, but rather to move into the dark, unknown aspects of the unconscious with the illuminating light of awareness.

For example, suppose you have a new job and are excited, relieved and happy. You are aware of these feelings (they are in the light of your awareness), yet you notice that you are experiencing insomnia, increased appetite and a sense of lethargy. As you explore your feelings more deeply, you find that fear, anger and resentment reside alongside the initial feelings of excitement, relief and happiness! An opportunity is presented for bringing the light of awareness into the feelings in the shadow. The feelings of excitement, happiness and relief could as easily have been in the shadow (unconscious), and fear, anger and resentment could have resided in the light (awareness). As all feelings are granted validity and allowed to advance into the light of awareness, they become powerful tools for supporting us through life's challenges.

The unconscious (shadow) releases necessary information to assist us in our growth process. Challenging feelings discharged from the shadow, such as fear, anger and resentment, act as warnings signaling us to pay attention to our needs. Our needs may be met by planning activities which more fully support our overall well-being, changing certain aspects of our lives, or having clearer, more honest communications. We become angry, fearful or resentful when our needs go unmet. Our effectiveness in taking care of our deeper, underlying requirements is dependent upon recognizing and honoring the full range of our feelings.

Holding our feelings in the unconscious realms of the shadow drains us of our energy and zaps our effectiveness. The types of feelings held in the shadow are inconsequential. Any and all feelings can be held captive. Thoughts or feelings we deny, reject, avoid or judge reside in the shadow and require our energy to remain hidden there. Our sexuality can live in the shadow when we suppress it, deny it, avoid it or judge it. Our complementary masculine or feminine aspect can end up in the shadow when we suppress it, deny it, avoid it or judge it. Awareness is the key for releasing the contents of the shadow. Knowledge is power. The more informed we are about all aspects of ourselves, the more effective we become.

KNOWLEDGE (LIGHT) IS EMPOWERING. LACK OF
KNOWLEDGE (DARKNESS) IS DISEMPOWERING.

Let us take this a step further. Suppose your next door neighbor is "Mr. Party-Hearty" and often plays very loud music into the wee hours of the morning. You find yourself experiencing anger and exhaustion and feeling violated, to the point where you are having murderous thoughts about your neighbor! Right now you may be thinking, "If I allow myself to have these murderous feelings, won't I be more likely to carry them out? Wouldn't it be better to keep those thoughts and feelings in the dark (the unknown of the shadow)?"

Initially, it may appear that *thinking* would lead to *doing;* however, exactly the opposite is true for most of us. Problems result when we suppress and fight our thoughts and feelings. In resisting them, we give our focus, power and energy to what we want to avoid. Remember, what we resist persists and grows. When we acknowledge, validate and allow our thoughts and feelings, we are much less likely to act inappropriately.

In this case you would have every right to be upset and angry with your noisy and inconsiderate neighbor. Your boundaries are being violated. To approach the problem in a level-headed manner requires allowing your feelings about your neighbor so that effective action may be taken. Once feelings are acknowledged and allowed, we become effective in selecting the appropriate actions to support and care for ourselves without harming others. You may decide to speak with him face-to face, form an alliance with other neighbors or become instrumental in passing a long-overdue noise ordinance in your area. Acknowledging and accepting your feelings is an imperative step in transforming the shadow to light. As we become aware, we can respond appropriately to life's challenges rather than react to the stimuli that life offers.

Our inherent wholeness includes acknowledging all aspects of ourselves, including the vast collection of our opposites and polarities. We each possess loving and less desirable attributes. We can be generous as well as selfish, energetic and lazy, happy as well as sad, compassionate and judgmental, bored and exhilarated, peaceful and warlike. Being human encompasses the entire spectrum of expression. When we embrace all aspects of ourselves, we transcend the limitations of fear and expand into our wholeness.

The Power of the Shadow

Feelings and thoughts that are denied, repressed and avoided accumulate in the unconscious mind (shadow). The accumulation of the unconscious aspects of ourselves build up over time and create a core of energy that takes on a life of its own. This collection of energy literally builds momentum to the point where our personalities can become quite volatile. If we have built up an energy core of unexpended feelings of sadness, a scene from a sad movie or a poignant experience of any sort may stimulate what feels like waves of uncontrollable sadness. Or perhaps we have feelings of anger, but because anger is considered an unacceptable emotion in our society, we suppress our feelings, which only makes the anger escalate into rage. When a seemingly innocuous incident occurs, such as an offhand comment or a misinterpreted look, the rage can come spewing out at volcanic speed and intensity. We feel out of control when such incidents occur, and we try even harder to regain control by suppressing our feelings. This only stokes the fires of the inner battle.

The more we deny, suppress or avoid our feelings, the more likely this compressed energy builds and floods our psyches. We feel powerless as a result of this outpouring. On the physical level, the build-up of energy may manifest as illness. Research has documented that rage and hostility (pent-up anger) play a role in a person's susceptibility to heart disease.

How We Maintain the Contents of the Shadow

There are many ways we hold feelings and thoughts captive in the shadow (the unconscious). The three most common methods are denial, repression and projection.

(1) Denial

We are in denial when we do not tell the truth about ourselves to ourselves. The ultimate denial for many of us began when we were children. We may have been straightforward and outspoken about what we experienced and what we knew to be true. As we discovered that the adults in our lives found this behavior unacceptable, we stopped being open and honest in order to fit in and be loved. We became what we were not and said "No" to the truth of who we were. Denial becomes habitual with time.

(2) Repression

Carl Jung, world-renowned Swiss psychiatrist, believed that repression starts as intentional suppression. When fear, doubt or a troubling thought causes us to say inwardly, "No, let's not think about it," "It can't be," "I must be wrong," repression can occur. We do whatever it takes to shove the troublesome thought or feeling out of the conscious mind. The unacceptable thought or feeling is pushed down out of awareness as often as necessary to keep it hidden. Repression results when our troubling thoughts and feelings are safely concealed in the darkness.

(3) Projection

As previously discussed in Chapter Three, projection is the transference of our unclaimed self-perceptions onto another. We refuse to perceive and acknowledge an aspect of ourselves while clearly observing this characteristic in another person. Most projection is unconscious. Through the power of our belief systems (remember, we like to be right), it appears from all outward appearances that our perceptions are correct in regard to another. We often gather agreement from other people around us to feel even more justified in our perceptions (projections).

For example, when we admire a particular attribute of another person, such as their intellect, humor or beauty, we step out of darkness into the light of awareness as we acknowledge we also possess the admired quality. Conversely, when we are critical of another, we are projecting our unowned agenda onto another. We turn the darkness of unawareness into light when we acknowledge that we share the same limitations. We can only observe in others what dwells within us, both the grandness and the shortcomings. Others serve as mirrors for us—always.

As you see him, you will see yourself.
As you treat him, you will treat yourself.
As you think of him, you will think of yourself.
Never forget this, for in him you will
find yourself or lose yourself.

From A *Course in Miracles*

Paying attention to the people and things we dislike can inform us about the contents of our shadows. If Jane views June's sexual affair with disgust, it is likely that a part of Jane's sexuality is in the shadow and she is projecting her unresolved sexuality issues onto June. If Steve cannot tolerate Sam and says, "he's not a real man" because Sam does not enjoy sports, there is a good chance that Steve is projecting his unresolved masculinity issues onto Sam. If Camille cannot stand Cameron, the president of the organization to which she belongs because he "lords it over everybody," then Camille has likely projected her unresolved issues regarding power onto Cameron.

We are particularly sensitive to the traits in others that are buried within the shadows of our own unconscious. Ariana finds it difficult to deal with pompous (self-important) people. Her discomfort indicates she has not yet dealt with her feelings of inadequacy. Annaliese's blood boils whenever she encounters abuse of any kind. Her anger and fear suggest she has unresolved issues of abuse lurking in the shadows of her past.

With a sense of adventurous curiosity as our guide, we discover the hidden aspects of ourselves most clearly. An attitude of playfulness and wonder deters the critical voice from stepping in with its messages about what we should or should not think and feel and allows us to explore our hidden realms without hindrance. We delve deeply while stepping lightly with curiosity leading the way.

Each one of us possesses the same power as Beauty in taming our inner beasts. Transforming the beast within ourselves (the dark, hidden and unknown aspects) into a handsome Prince or Princess (the light of awareness) requires acknowledging and allowing the full range of human expression.

Love and acceptance provides the impetus for magic and transformation!

THE BEAST BECOMES "BEAUTY-FULL"
THROUGH ACCEPTANCE.

Retrieving the Shadow

All fear-based thoughts and feelings carry a message, a gift, if we are willing to perceive it. The gift of the shadow's message is to direct us toward specific needs that require attention. Insights leading to transformation occur when we allow expression of all our thoughts and feelings. In denying our thoughts and feelings, our true selves are denied. Denial wreaks havoc in our mind/body systems and, with time, physical ailments and even disease can become our experience. It is necessary to integrate (grant validity to) the unowned, shadow aspects of ourselves. Remember, it is not necessary to change a troubling thought or feeling. Our responsibility is to simply feel it and allow it to be. Consciously experiencing all that we feel empowers us to effectively ascertain our true needs.

When we ignore, invalidate and suppress the unresolved feelings residing in the shadow, they become destructive as they attempt to make themselves known. Allowing ourselves to become aware of the contents of the unconscious requires courage and the commitment to face our vulnerabilities. Most of us have become adept at keeping both the positive and negative aspects of the shadow hidden from ourselves and the world. It can feel threatening to bring those dark pieces of ourselves into the light of awareness. Revealing our inner darkness expands the comfort zone and will likely feel uncomfortable until the comfort zone adapts. It may be helpful to remember that disclosing the contents of the shadow is not about discovering what is wrong, but rather an exercise in uncovering what is. Exposing the shadow to the light is the equivalent of becoming en-lightened!!!

He who knows others is wise; he who knows himself is enlightened.

Lao-tzu

AN EXERCISE FOR DISCOVERING THE NEEDS OF THE SHADOW

We recommend that you read the contents of the entire exercise before you begin. This exercise is most effective when practiced in solitude, accompanied by soft, soothing music and deep, slow breathing.

Step One
Relax and close your eyes. Use your imagination to conceptualize yourself and the immediate space around you as consisting of an invisible circle of awareness, a circle of light.

Step Two
Imagine that the personalities of your shadow-self reside in the darkness outside of your circle of light. You and your circle of light are surrounded by the many personality aspects that inhabit your unconscious.

Step Three
Bring to mind an area of your personal life in which you are currently experiencing challenge. This area could be your health, your anger, your sadness, your sense of powerlessness, your

self-doubt, your lack of worth—any area that you feel creates a sense of difficulty. This is a piece of your shadow.

Step Four

Invite this piece of your shadow into your circle of light. Allow yourself to fully experience the presence of this intriguing visitor. As you imagine that this visitor from the shadow can communicate with you, ask, "What is it that you need?" Listen quietly and respectfully to the response it gives. The response from the shadow aspect may be presented to you with pictures, words, feelings or images. Allow yourself enough time to investigate the feelings that accompany your messages as you perform this exercise. Acknowledge every answer you receive with a "thank you." When you would like more information, ask, "What else do you need?" Continue to make inquiries into the needs of your shadow personality until you feel complete.

Step Five

Slowly bring your focus back to your surroundings and open your eyes. Have a notebook ready to record the messages and insights you received. Be gentle with yourself and allow yourself the time necessary to assimilate the information from your shadow aspects. As you feel ready, take the actions that are necessary to complete this process of turning knowledge into wisdom.

This is a powerful exercise when we allow ourselves to open fully to the personalities of our deeper, hidden selves. In the unveiling of the dark aspects, we may find that we are faced with messages that are challenging. This presents an opportunity to be open, to trust that this is the right time to discover whatever is revealed. If we were not ready to receive this information, it would not present itself to us. Remember, we are delving into the unconscious. Its contents can be inspiring, challenging, surprising and unexpected.

Performing this exercise on a regular basis provides the mechanism to uncover the essential elements of life's challenges. We move from living in the dark into the light of awareness—from ineffectiveness to empowerment. Over time we develop greater trust in our inner resources as we tap into the deeper recesses of the psyche. The keys that allow growth are trust, patience, allowance and persistence. We invite you to freely and abundantly give yourself these gifts of awareness!

Ariana performed the above exercise as she was preparing to leave her full-time job to pursue her passion for writing and teaching. She resolved to use her fears about leaving her job to her advantage rather than be overwhelmed by them. She invited the personality aspect of her fears into her circle of light and was given this response: "I'm afraid of you leaving your job because then you will become more of who you are—outspoken and outrageous! How will I protect you and take care of you? You will no longer remain behind the scenes; you'll be out in the world. This scares me."

The fears that her shadow aspect voiced were real and valid for her. Yes, her life would certainly change in leaving behind the comfort of the known in the form of the job she had held for many years. She realized her fear was looking out for her best interest. Its purpose was not to keep her from quitting her job and moving forward, but to assist her in taking care of herself in this transitional phase of her life.

The fear's message strongly influenced the way in which Ariana pursued her goal. She chose to take her time as she made the transition from her job to her new ventures. She made an agreement with herself that she would approach every step in a self-honoring way. She built a loving support system around her consisting of family and friends. She allowed the outspoken and outrageous aspects of herself to evolve slowly so as not to create undue stress upon her psyche. Her transition into her new life went smoothly as a result of regarding the fears of her shadow.

Communicating with the thoughts, feelings and symptoms that live in the shadow creates the opportunity for expanded perspectives and a deepened awareness of our essential self. This is an on-going process. The purpose of our encounters with the dark is not to rid ourselves of the feeling, thought or symptom but rather to promote balance, peace of mind and integration. Old wounds are healed. We reside at a higher level of wholeness. This is life lived passionately and fully.

Dreams—Messengers of the Unconscious

One does not become enlightened by imagining figures of light, but by making the darkness conscious.

Carl Jung

Carl Jung believed that all phases of our nature are revealed in dreams for the purpose of directing us to higher, more balanced accomplishments in our physical, mental and spiritual life. Dreams are a powerful way to become aware of what is in the shadow. Everyone dreams, yet many people find it difficult to remember their dreams. Some dismiss their dreams as nonsense. Dreams are significant to each and every one of us as they provide the inroads to our deeper, truer nature.

Erich Fromm in his book, *The Forgotten Language, says, ...if all our dreams were pleasant phantasmagorias in which our hearts' wishes were fulfilled, we might feel friendlier toward them. But many of them leave us in an anxious mood; often they are nightmares from which we awake gratefully acknowledging that we only dreamed. Others, though not nightmares, are disturbing for other reasons. They do not fit the person we are sure we are during the daytime. We dream of hating people whom we believe we are fond of, of loving someone whom we thought we had no interest in. We dream of being ambitious, when we are convinced of being modest; we dream of bowing down and submitting, when we are so proud of our independence. But worse than all is the fact that we do not understand our dreams while we, the waking person, are sure we can understand anything if we put our minds to it. Rather than be confronted with such overwhelming proof of the limitations of our understanding, we accuse the dreams of not making sense.*

Our dream state allows unresolved situations, feelings and thoughts to be presented in such a way that they are acceptable to our awake minds. The dream imagery may seem bizarre, even ridiculous, yet unacceptable aspects of our shadow self are made available to our conscious minds through our dreams.

Recently, Annaliese dreamed that she tried to destroy two women—one woman was blond (light) and represented the positive attributes of Annaliese, the other woman was brunette (dark) and represented her negative aspects. As she was hiding the women (hiding both the light and dark aspects from herself), a neighbor woman appeared (another aspect of Annaliese's psyche). The neighbor insisted that something of value was thrown away in the exact vicinity where Annaliese had attempted to hide the dark-haired woman (the dark side has value). This dream clearly suggests to Annaliese that a great deal of integration remains concerning accepting both the dark and the light aspects of herself.

Dreams are critical to emotional health and can be therapeutic. Even dreams that are not remembered create an impact upon our psyche which allows us to work through difficult circumstances from our waking lives. Through our dreams the unconscious mind connects with our outer world in a way that would seem impossible in our waking state. Dreams assist us in the detection of and solution to problems which baffle the conscious mind.

Ariana dreamt she was going to visit a friend at a farm. Upon her arrival at her friend's farm, she noticed her hair was messy, and as she got out of her car, she stepped into a pile of manure! She cleaned the manure from her shoes as best she could and proceeded up the walk to her friend's house.

The friend appeared at the door, clad in her bathrobe. Clearly uncomfortable with Ariana's visit, the friend said that she could not visit now because it was nearly supper time. Returning to her car, Ariana noticed futuristic pipe fittings lying on the grounds of the farm.

When Ariana awoke, she contemplated the dream's meaning. She intuited that the symbolism of the dream carried an important message for her. She realized it was time to move out of her manure (her self-doubt) and alter her thinking (represented by the messy hair) about her ability to write and teach from her intuitive self (symbolized by the futuristic pipeline connected to the Source). The dream signified the inner doubts she had been harboring about her professional capa-bilities. After contemplating the meaning of her dream, she drifted off to sleep and saw herself standing among a large group of people who were very pleased and were applauding her for understanding the message of her dream!

Sometimes dreams are predictive, giving us information about the future which our conscious minds are unable to ac-cess. Annaliese's neighbor (not the neighbor in her dream) dreamt she had a lump in her right breast. The next morning as she was brushing her hair, she remembered her dream. She put her hand on her right breast and discovered the lump she had experienced in her dream. Our dreams provide a connec-tion between the wisdom of the unconscious (shadow) self and our conscious, awake minds. Important messages are re-layed from our inner world to the outer world through dreams.

Another form of predictive dreams is the experience com-monly referred to as déjà vu. When we encounter a sense of familiarity, as if we have previously experienced a conversa-tion, person or place (déjà vu), a predictive dream is often the cause. We may feel as if we have already spoken and heard the words of the conversation in which we are engaging, or we know we have seen a place before, even though we are cer-tain we have never been there. These and other examples are often the result of predictive dreams. Most predictive dreams are about everyday occurrences and are not as dramatic as finding a lump in the breast.

Dream Interpretation Guidelines

Dream Characters

We each play every part in our dreams, even the "bad guys." Dream characters primarily represent aspects of ourselves.

Occasionally our dreams relate to family, friends, lovers and events in our world. Our dream characters' appearance, voice inflections, facial expressions, gestures and apparel are significant as each detail adds to the meaning of the dream and completes the message.

Signs and Messages

The signs and messages of dreams are literal, indicating their exact meaning. If John has a dream in which he sees himself at a barber shop with the accompanying message "get a haircut tomorrow," the dream's meaning is likely just that—go get a haircut tomorrow.

Dream Symbols: Verbal and Visual Puns

It may be easy to confuse the signals and messages dreams provide with dream symbols. Sometimes dream symbols are composed of verbal or visual puns. If John's dream was of Wild West Indians ready to scalp him, the symbolism of scalping provides a potentially important message. Being scalped could be a play on words that refers to a fear lurking in the shadows of John's unconscious regarding a business matter.

Expanded Meanings of Dream Symbols

The symbols and messages in dreams are comprised of our own unique life experiences. We dream in symbols because we think in symbols at the conscious level. For example, when Shawna dreams of her husband Bruce, she will likely view his face rather than hear or say his name. The symbols of our dreams possess expanded meanings. A house, for example, can symbolize a variety of daily activities and often represents our emotional, mental, physical and spiritual states. If we dream of food or kitchens, these symbols may represent sustenance and nurturing. A bathroom may represent cleansing or purging. The bedroom may represent sexuality or being at rest. All dream symbols vary with the individual and may change meaning with the variation of inner emotional states and life circumstances.

Dreams assist us in confronting current challenges and becoming aware of unfamiliar circumstances. Utilized to their full extent, the messages of dreams provide a powerful instrument for revealing our inner truths to ourselves.

EXERCISE: REMEMBERING DREAMS

Dreams are like memories, they're easy to lose.

Uncle Arthur, from *Unstrung Heroes*

There are many of us who think we do not dream because we have no memory of them. We all dream. The following are suggestions for remembering dreams:

1) Place a pen and notebook by your bed. As you awaken, immediately record the symbols, feelings and thoughts you experienced in your dreams.

2) Make a conscious intention to recall your dreams. Our conscious intentions carry much power. Our conscious and unconscious mind will respond to our proposed intentions with regular practice.

3) Enlist the support of others as well as books on the subject of dream interpretation. An objective viewpoint is often necessary for discovering the meanings of symbols in our dreams.

4) When a dream is encountered that makes no sense initially, allow time for the meaning to unfold. Forcing

meanings upon our dream symbols renders dream interpretation ineffectual. Dreams hold the potential of showing us how to care for ourselves more effectively in every part of our lives.

When we include both the light (aware) and the dark (shadow) aspects of ourselves in our journey, our lives are immeasurably enriched. The shadow grants us the opportunity to reveal our vitality, creativity, zest and adventure. Our intrinsic nature is uncovered through exploring the dark recesses of our psyches. The darkness of the earth, the darkness of the womb, the dark cave, the dark depth of the oceans all nurture life, growth and creativity. Conscious awareness, the vehicle through which we create the experience of our lives, comes to us from the dark, shadowy confines of the unconscious.

It requires courage to move into the depths of the shadow. Most of us avoid the unknown and refrain from exploring our fears. Our wholeness becomes evident as we allow our belief systems to accommodate and accept the dark, shadowy aspects of ourselves as a blessing-in-waiting.

Blessed are the men and women who are planted
on your earth in your garden
who grow as your trees and flowers grow,
who transform their darkness to light.
Their roots plunge into darkness;
Their faces turn toward the light.

Song of Solomon, translated by Stephen Mitchell

BE AT PEACE

FOR YOU ARE GREATLY LOVED

6

JOY AND PAIN

Here in this body are the sacred rivers: here are the sun and moon as well as all the pilgrimage places.... I have not encountered another temple as blissful as my own body.

Saraha

The Quest for Happiness

It is natural to desire the best possible experiences and circumstances in life. As we undertake the fulfillment of our desires, we give ourselves and the world the message: "I matter, I value myself, and I deserve to have what I want!" The desire to experience the elements of contentment such as security, pleasure, fulfillment and love lives within all of us. We could sum up the variations of these commonly held desires by calling them "the desire to be happy." For many, happiness is associated with the physical conditions of life and is assumed to be synonymous with joy.

The following examples contain an underlying assumption which suggests that if we attain certain physical circumstances, happiness will automatically follow:

"I wish I had more money (then I'd be happy)."
"If only I were healthier (then I'd be happy)."
"I'd like to quit this job and find a better one (then I'd
be happy)."
"I wish I could find Mr./Ms. Right (then I'd be happy)."
"If I could just lose this extra weight (then I'd be happy)."

Happiness, as the above examples demonstrate, becomes dependent upon the outer physical circumstances of life.

Regardless of the form our wants and desires take, whether it is a new job, losing weight, forming a significant relationship, buying a new home, or being healthy, they all share one common motivator: *the desire for an enhanced experience of life!* Hidden beneath the outward, physical manifestation of our desires, often at an unconscious level, lies the true purpose of our longings—the longing for happiness. We are all motivated by the quest for happiness.

Many of us have learned from experience that the attainment of physical desires does not guarantee happiness. When we are unhappy, our tendency is to search for solutions outside of ourselves by going after what we consider to be the next missing element in our lives. "My new relationship isn't all I had hoped for. I think I will leave my partner and concentrate on getting my degree (then I'll be happy)." "I have this great new sports car and I still don't feel wild and sexy like I thought I would. Maybe I should break up with my fiancée and start dating again (then I'll be happy)." "I've moved into my new home but I feel unsettled. Maybe I'll take out a loan for landscaping (then I'll be happy)." And the search goes on.

The incessant pursuit for the next desire in our lives, and the next, comes from the belief that we will be happy only when we acquire certain possessions and circumstances—and not before. This makes the experience of happiness conditional, temporary and elusive.

In our hunger for happiness we have been operating without awareness. Since physical conditions and circumstances in and of themselves do not provide true and lasting happiness, how can we effectively acquire the most sought-after goal of the human experience—happiness?

Is Happiness the Same as Joy?

We do not become happy because we get what we want; we get what we want because we choose happiness first.

Alan Cohen, *Joy Is My Compass*

We think of joy as being the equivalent of happiness and pain as being akin to sorrow. In truth, they are neither. Joy is not based upon conditional circumstances. Joy is a state of BEING and is experienced by living fully in the moment. Slowing down the hectic pace of our lives to be cognizant of the beauty of a flower, the smile of a child, the feeling of surprise when our ice cream falls out of the cone onto the sidewalk grounds us in the present and supports the experience of joy. Allowing each moment to be sufficient as it is without the need to change it or assess it as wrong or right means we are living in the timeless here and now. When we allow ourselves to live in the present, we live "happily ever after."

No person or thing outside of ourselves can make us happy (or sad or angry). We are the ultimate source of our experiences. Taking ownership of this fact can prove to be a life-changing endeavor.

Pain—the Ultimate Form of Resistance

Pain is the result of resisting life's experiences. The pain of resistance is created by getting caught up in judgment. When we experience the pain our resistance brings, our life's focus becomes the avoidance of misery rather than the expression of joy. As we move through resistance to life's experiences, we allow the full range of feelings including anger, grief, jealousy, greed and hostility, among other "unacceptable" feelings. When we embrace our feelings, allow their expression and are accountable for them, energy flows unimpeded through our bodies and we release the resistance which creates the experience of pain.

Suppressing, denying or projecting our feelings causes pain because energy does not flow. When we acknowledge and allow our feelings, a transformation occurs which permits pain to shift to joy. With this shift from pain to joy the energy of love and harmony flows freely, affecting every cell in our body. The only barrier between ourselves and joy is resistance to our experiences.

AN EXERCISE FOR TRANSFORMING PAIN TO JOY

The next time you feel upset, dissatisfied, frustrated, stressed or out of balance, here is an experiment to try. Instead of finding a distraction in an attempt to feel better, such as reading, watching television, logging on the computer or eating, find a quiet place where you can turn inward and observe yourself. Notice your breathing; is it shallow and fast? Concentrate on filling your lungs fully, slowly and deeply. The breath assists us in becoming centered and focused. As you breathe, allow yourself to be quiet and still. In the stillness of your breathing, simply observe your thoughts and feelings. Do not attempt to change them, fix them or make yourself right or wrong. Simply be the observer of your inner life. Allow your experience to become the center of your world for this short period of time. Just watch and breathe. If judgments of yourself or others arise, notice them and let them go.

This is a simple method for transforming resistance to allowance, pain to joy. The more this exercise is used, the more joy becomes our experience of life.

The degree to which we allow ourselves to *feel* affects the totality of our emotional and physical experiences. Our thoughts, feelings and beliefs have a profound effect upon the body through the interactions of the brain with all other bodily systems. A new science called psychoneuroimmunology (PNI) is finding that our psychological characteristics—thoughts, feelings and personality—are conveyed through our neurological anatomy (the brain and nervous system). Our thoughts, feelings and personality affect our immunological defenses and, ultimately, our health. Many scientists suggest that there is no separation between our bodies and our minds. We are a "mind/body system."

THE BELIEFS WE HAVE ABOUT OURSELVES AND THE WORLD INFLUENCE OUR HEALTH THROUGH THE MIND/ BODY CONNECTION.

The Mind/Body Connection

We all tend to think of our bodies as *"frozen sculptures"—solid, fixed, material objects—when in truth they are more like rivers, constantly changing, flowing patterns of intelligence.*

Dr. Deepak Chopra, *Quantum Healing*

Human beings are comprised primarily of various forms of energy. Quantum physicists have found that our bodies are mostly empty space. As a matter of fact, our bodies are 99.999% empty space! The body consists of energy and atoms. Atoms are particles whirling at lightning speed through vast, empty spaces. They are minute fluctuations of energy in the infinite expanse of energy called the "unified field." It is from the unified field that all natural forces emerge, including our bodies.

Most of us are not aware of the inner workings of quantum reality. Our experience of physical reality is limited by our five senses: seeing, hearing, touching, feeling and smelling. These five senses are so finely attuned that we experience our world as very dense, solid and finite. Yet many things exist which cannot be perceived with the naked eye—atoms, viruses, cells, magnetics and electricity to name a few. These "unseen" examples of reality are forms of energy. We are able to see and experience only the results of these unseen energies with our bodies' sensing mechanisms. Our five senses are limited in the perception of the many forms of subtle, refined energies.

Our Bodies Are in a State of Constant Change

The Greek philosopher Heraclitus declared, "You cannot step into the same river twice." Fresh waters are constantly flowing into the river. The same is true of our bodies. The fat on our bodies is not the same as it was last month—fat cells are replaced every three weeks. We acquire a new stomach lining every five days. (The innermost cells of the stomach are replaced in a matter of minutes as we digest food.) Our skin is renewed every five weeks. The skeletons of our bodies, which seem so stable and fixed, are entirely new every three months. We appear to be the same outside, yet we are like a beautiful garden whose colors are continuously being altered and rearranged. Science has confirmed these ongoing physical bodily changes. The quantum (smallest possible building block of energy) level of the mind/body system controls this constant state of fluctuation.

What chemical reactions occur within our physical bodies to create ongoing change? Every thought and feeling activates receptors in the brain which secrete messenger chemicals throughout the body. These chemicals set off a multitude of reactions. Our immune cells, for example, hear our every thought and feeling via the activity of the messenger chemicals produced by the brain. Every cell of our body is constantly in communication with all other cells via messenger molecules. The immune system communicates the invasion of a flu virus to the brain. The brain, along with messenger molecules throughout the body, sets in motion the activity of natural killer cells which, under ideal conditions, destroy the virus. Our bodies are comprised of a natural flow of dynamic energy which is interconnected and self-regulating.

The Influence of Beliefs and Feelings Upon the Body

Bill Moyers reported in his television special, *Healing and the Mind*, on a study done with method-trained actors. These actors possess the capacity to call upon their own personal memories and experiences to generate the intense emotional states necessary to act realistically.

The method actors in the study improvised a monologue which provoked both happy and sad emotions. Their immune systems were measured to determine what changes, if any, transpired during the intense feelings of happiness and sadness. It was discovered that there was an increase in the number of natural killer cells in the actors' bloodstreams during both happy and sad states, and that these cells were functioning more effectively during those highly emotional periods than when the actors were in a neutral state of emotion.

This study supports what science has been postulating for several years: We are a mind/body system which operates most effectively when we give our feelings expression. Resisting our feelings is detrimental to the immune system and predisposes us to disease. Energy flows freely when we experience *all* of our feelings, enhancing the health of our immune system and contributing to our over-all well-being.

The healing system is the way the body mobilizes all its resources to combat disease. The belief system is often the activator of the healing system.

Norman Cousins

Our Bodies Possess Built-In Intelligence

Each cell in our body possesses innate *intelligence*. This nonmeasurable, nonphysical, built-in intelligence works in partnership with all of the communicator molecules throughout the mind/body system. Our bodies' innate intelligence has the capacity to transform chaos into order. Its properties are superior to any external substitution such as chemical drugs. Deepak Chopra, M.D., believes that this intelligence "has to come from somewhere and that somewhere may be everywhere."

The mind/body system is a "network of information." Every cell is capable of sending and receiving an immeasurable quantity of messages. In the past, humans were considered to be nothing more than a body machine with the mind (intellect) confined only to the brain. With the increased awareness that science offers today, we can say we are a living intelligence that has learned to create a physical machine— the body.

How is it possible that our minds, comprised of thought, emotion, perception, memory, imagination and spirit, so profoundly affect our bodies? The human is an indivisible whole and the mind inhabits the entirety of the body. The mind, with its intelligence, dwells within the skin, the organs, the muscles, the skeletal structure and every cell of the body. There is no place in the body where the mind does not reside. The immune system and the mind communicate with each other through a constant flow of biochemical messages. Each message contains a particular combination of molecules that matches a specific receptor similar to the way a key fits a lock. Healthy messenger molecules recognize and destroy invaders by latching onto their receptors. In this way the body fights disease. This ongoing inner communication and self-regulation process most frequently transpires without symptoms of illness or conscious awareness on our part.

Neuropeptides—Messengers of Emotion

In the 1970s, research studies began which made a strong impact upon mind/body science. A method was discovered to measure "endorphins" and their receptors. Structurally endorphins are "neuropeptides," members of a network which links thoughts, feelings and beliefs to health.

Neuropeptides are released from the hypothalamus into the pituitary gland which regulates dozens of bodily processes, including the release of fight-or-flight stress hormones. Neuropeptides frequently mimic the action of mood-altering drugs. They are found in the limbic system of the brain which influences our drives and emotions. These messenger molecules exert a powerful reaction upon our emotional responses. "Each emotion might be the result of a unique combination of neuropeptides," says Candace Pert, Ph.D.

Pert and other researchers suggest that neuropeptides may be the "biochemicals of emotions." Neurobiologists have found neuropeptides and their receptors inhabiting all organs of the body, including the intestinal lining. This gives a broader overview of the expression "gut feeling." Through the neuropeptide system, people may very well experience feelings in their guts. The intelligence of the mind, by means of the neuropeptide system, resides in every cell of our bodies.

The discovery of neuropeptides suggests that the body possesses fluidity, as does the mind. Since neuropeptides influence the entire body, the many various parts of our body can "think" and "feel" in the sense that they are capable of producing the same neuropeptides that originate in the brain. Neuropeptides serve as a point of transformation between the nonphysical (nonmatter) and the physical (matter). They are the bridges connecting thoughts and feelings with physical reactions within the body. When someone bumps into you with their shopping cart in the supermarket, you may experience pain followed by anger. The pain and anger your body has experienced will travel along a nerve to the brain and are transformed into a neurochemical that spreads through the mind/body system. Nonmatter becomes matter through the workings of neuropeptides.

Our Emotional States Influence Health

What affects one part of the mind/body, affects all of the mind/body. Researchers have produced evidence that suggests our emotional states influence the immune system. Current studies show that people who have recently lost spouses are themselves more likely to die within the following year. Ongoing depression leads to biological changes which can negatively affect the immune system. (Grief, on the other hand, does not create the same negative reactions within the immune system as depression does). Researchers have recently discovered a neurotransmitter in depressed people called an "imipramine." Imipramine is abnormally produced in the brains of depressed people. Receptors for the neurotransmitter imipramine were found not only in the brain, but also in other cells of the body suggesting a depressed person can have depressed skin, a depressed liver, a depressed heart, and so on.

When all emotions are allowed healthy expression, the mind/body control system is enhanced so that the immune system is strengthened and the disease process is less likely to occur. The health of the immune system thrives when we are living in the truth of each moment. Internal balance is the key to health. Whenever we repress or project our thoughts and feelings or express them in a violent manner, an internal war is launched within our mind/body systems. This internal war is at the root of many diseases.

NEGLECTED ASPECTS OF OURSELVES BECOME TOXIC
ONLY WHEN THEY ARE NOT ALLOWED EXPRESSION.

Health and Healing

The primitive health-regulating portion of the brain where emotional states are processed does not utilize language as we know it (right brain function). Language is the main tool of the rational cortex portion of the brain which formulates information (left brain function). This makes communication between the cortex and the primitive brain difficult. As a consequence, most people cannot easily control the health-regulating portions of the brain merely through thoughts, words and ideas.

Interestingly enough, the primitive brain may be accessed in ways the rational brain may not easily comprehend. We can bypass the rational, thinking portion of the brain by attaining altered states of consciousness through meditation, drumming, dance, ritual, dreaming and hypnosis. These and other mechanisms allow us to move beyond the rational functions of the left brain into the deeper right brain centers associated with emotions and regulation of the health of the body.

MEDITATION, IMAGERY AND RELAXATION TECHNIQUES
EFFECTIVELY QUIET THE BUSY, THINKING CORTEX CEN-
TER OF THE BRAIN SO THE CALMING, HEALING CENTERS
OF THE BRAIN ARE ACTIVATED.

Health means "to make whole, to bring together." Wholeness is associated with integrity, completeness, totality and oneness. Because health is our natural state, there is a natural, inner tendency within our bodies to move toward wholeness.

There is a difference between curing and healing. Effecting a cure is the primary focus of traditional medicine. Curing occurs when a person comes to a physician with a broken bone or a wound that requires stitching. Traditional medicine does not generate the healing of the wound. It can only create the conditions under which the tissue can knit back together and repair itself. Actual healing takes place in another domain.

Healing is a function of inner resources originating within the mind/body system, the point where the natural intelligence of the body takes effect. Each of us possesses the resources necessary for healing any given physical ailment. The healing process is an internal one.

Modern medicine assists by aiding the patient in surviving the symptoms of illness. The mind/body's natural system of balance which promotes healing is then allowed to take hold. Deepak Chopra, in his book *Quantum Healing*, says, "If you can successfully restore balance to the mind/body, then the patient's immune system will respond."

There are many levels of healing: physical healing (the focus of traditional medicine), emotional healing, mental healing and spiritual healing. Healing can occur on one of these levels without taking place on others. For instance, a person can heal on a physical level but not on an emotional, mental or spiritual level. Another person may heal on an emotional level but not on a physical level. Traditional medicine assumes it has failed whenever a person is not healed on a physical level.

SCIENCE HAS SHOWN THAT THE BODY AND MIND ARE LIKE PARALLEL WORLDS. ANYTHING THAT OCCURS IN THE MENTAL WORLD LEAVES FOOTPRINTS IN THE PHYSICAL ONE. OUR BODIES ARE A REFLECTION OF ALL THAT WE THINK AND FEEL.

The Gift of Illness

The longer I am sick the more I realize that illness is to health what dreams are to waking life—the reminder of what is forgotten, the bigger picture working toward resolution.

Kat Duff, *The Alchemy of Illness*

The condition of illness lives in the dark, shadowlands of life, threatening us with yet another element to fear or ignore. Illness evokes a sense of powerlessness and brings to our awareness the frailty and vulnerability of our human bodies. We lie humbled and prostrate at the feet of illness, uncertain of the ongoing process of life.

All illness offers us the unique gift of further exploring the domains of the shadow self where our unrecalled memories, experiences and feelings lie. Illness often manifests as a mechanism to recollect memories from the past so that they may be integrated into our current understanding of who we are.

We do not create our illnesses from a lack of awareness or some other downfall with which we are plagued. Instead, illness provides an opportunity to heal on any given level of our human experience: physical, emotional, and/or spiritual. As Kat Duff states in her book, *The Alchemy of Illness*, "...illness can function to compensate for onesidedness, reestablish equilibrium, and allow new solutions to evolve, on a metabolic level as well as the psychological, *one could say it is a call for self-realization*." (Authors' emphasis)

Illness and other imbalances of the mind/body create the opportunity for opening to our inner world and reflecting upon the changes required to reestablish balance. Illness provides the mechanism for eliminating toxins from our physical, mental and emotional bodies.

Healing Dynamics

Health is not some kind of static thing that you grab and run with to the goal line. Health is a dynamic energy flow that changes over a lifetime. In fact, health and illness very often coexist together.

Jon Kabat-Zinn, Ph.D., *Wherever You Go, There You Are*

Healing is not so much about getting better as it is about letting go of everything that is not inherently yours. Releasing the expectations, the beliefs and the fears that do not serve you allows you to express more fully the truth of who you are. Not a better you—a more *authentic* you.

Health can be thought of as a balance between natural forces within the body. Adjusting the balance among physical, emotional, mental and spiritual variables promotes health. Balance is established and maintained by accepting, allowing and expressing all of our feelings and judgments—*joy.* This promotes the smooth flow of chemicals within the body which assists the vibrancy of the immune system. Imbalances of the mind/body contribute to disease. Imbalances are created when we resist our experiences, thereby setting in motion a flood of chemicals which inhibit the body's ability to cleanse itself of toxins, which in turn contribute to the onset of disease—*pain.*

The sorrows, joys, fleeting seconds of trauma, and long hours of nothing special at all silently accumulate and, like grains of sand deposited by a river, the minutes can eventually pile up into a hidden formation that crops above the surface as disease.

Deepak Chopra, *Quantum Healing*

How We Get From Here To There—Imbalance To Balance

Part of being a healthy person is being well integrated and at peace, with all of the systems acting together.

Candace Pert, Ph.D.

Obtaining balance is the key to optimum health.   The following topics delve into areas which support the creation of balance in life.

Working Effectively with Stress

Stress is a fact of life. Our modern-day living environment is filled with demands, expectations, hustle and bustle, schedules to keep, and energy-intensive activity. What to do?! The dynamics of stress are well documented: The heart and breathing rates increase, blood sugar levels rise and the blood from the digestive system moves to the large muscles. These symptoms are indicative of the built-in "fight-or-flight" mechanism for survival.   The chemicals released from the fight-or-flight response can turn toxic within the body without a healthy outlet for their release.

In the past it was agreed that "Type A" personalities were most prone to the adverse effects of stress. Recent research has shown that the hurry-up, impatient characteristics of the Type A person are not as caustic to the body as the hostile personality. (Certain Type A traits have now been proven to promote health.) Hostility, defined as barely controlled anger surging through the body, has proven to be dangerous to the health of the heart and the body in general. Hostility occurs as a result of suppressing anger until it erupts. Frequent waves of hostile anger raise the level of stress chemicals which damage the heart and increase cholesterol levels to dangerous highs. Hostility alone has been shown to predict our susceptibility to heart disease.

It has been further theorized that when emotions such as anger are not given expression (when they are repressed), they produce chemical changes in the body that weaken the immune system, thereby promoting the development of cancer. The label "Type C" describes people who tend to be overly understanding, compliant, stoic and uncomplaining—traits that may be to their detriment.

It is important to note that while personality influences health and disease, its effect is impacted by genetic and environmental factors as well. Rarely is a single element, psychological or otherwise, the single cause of disease. Utilizing the tools offered in *Journey Into Wholeness* contributes to good health, and does not necessarily inoculate us against disease. We express our wholeness through a commitment to experiencing life in a manner that is as full, complete and joyful as possible. Uncontrolled stress is one of the greatest inhibitors to our experience of wholeness. Given that stress and the many forms it takes are a fact of life, how do we stay healthy?

Here's a two-step formula for handling stress.
Step 1: Don't sweat the small stuff.
Step 2: Remember, it's all small stuff.

Anthony Robbins

The Three Cs

A study involving thousands of telephone company middle- and upper-management employees was undertaken in the 1970s. At that time, the telephone company was going through tremendous upheavals. The researchers who formulated the study, Kobasa and Maddi, shared a compelling question: Is there a difference in personality between people who remain healthy under high levels of stress and those who become ill under stress?

Thus began the initial research into a personality style termed "hardiness." The study of the relationship between personality and stress uncovered three attitudes specific to hardy people who did not succumb to illness under stress. The three attitudes are now called the "three Cs:" *commitment, control and challenge.*

Commitment

Hardy people are deeply *committed* to the quality of their lives. They possess a sense of purpose which is demonstrated in their intense involvement with the aspects of their lives that hold meaning for them. They are certain of the importance of their personal values, goals, capabilities and well-being.

Control

A sense of *control* strengthens the hardy personality with the self-trust necessary to influence the events of their lives. Their feeling of control comes from how they choose to respond to their experiences. They possess a sense of effectiveness in the face of change.

Challenge

The hardy personality views change as a *challenging* opportunity rather than a threat. They anticipate change as a normal occurrence of life, and view it as less stressful than the person lacking hardiness. They possess the ability to evaluate the impact of change from an overall life perspective.

We become more optimistic and powerful in our lives when we are *committed* to ourselves and the quality of our lives, when we feel in *control* of life's events and are *challenged* with the positive expectation of change. Utilizing the three Cs assists us in preventing feelings of helplessness, hopelessness and depression. We experience a deep sense of connectedness and belonging, sometimes referred to as "spirit."

The willingness to be accountable for our behavior, to feel and accept our feelings and to enlist the influence of spirit creates a powerful force for health.

Connectedness and Support

Researchers suspect that close, supportive relationships encourage health. A fourth "C" should be added to our list: *connectedness.* Studies show that people live longer who have strong, ongoing support from a marriage partner or good friend(s). Our mind/body requires communication and companionship with others for optimum health. Loneliness has a direct negative impact on the immune system. Sharing our deepest thoughts and feelings with others can decrease the effects of stress and strengthen our immune system.

Cardiologist Dean Ornish believes that isolation and loneliness are causative factors in creating the stress that leads to heart disease and other physical and emotional disorders. Ornish suggests that heart disease is in part a disease of the spirit, where there is a lack of connectedness to something larger than ourselves. Most of his patients experience a sense of isolation from their feelings, other people, their community and themselves. Heart disease has often been reversed in Ornish's patients by establishing healthy eating and exercise patterns, calming the mind and forming a strong system of support (connectedness).

A study was performed under the guidance of David Speigel, M.D., professor of Psychiatry and Behavioral Sciences at Stanford University of Medicine, with groups of women undergoing chemotherapy for breast cancer. The women who met with other women in Dr. Speigel's breast cancer support groups lived twice as long as women who had the same medical treatment but did not meet in the groups. The connectedness that accompanies support is proving to be effective "medicine."

Natural forces within us are the true healers of disease.

Hippocrates

Relaxation and Meditation

Relaxation and meditation techniques contribute to establishing and maintaining balance within our mind/body.

Meditation, visualization and biofeedback are tools which reduce stress, invoke inner calm, aid in relaxation and alter bodily processes. We move from our involvement with the outer world into the safe, quiet recesses of the inner world. Relaxation and meditative techniques require dedication, patience and practice. These skills bring calmness, the ability to focus, inner control and self-mastery, all which enhance the quality of life. In the relaxed condition, we enter an altered state of consciousness long associated with healing.

The relaxed physiological condition achieved in meditation is separate and distinct from the state of rest or sleep. Our bodies' energy reserves rebuild and the fight-or-flight response actually seems to shift into reverse. The heart rate decreases, breathing becomes slower and shallower and blood pressure decreases. While in the state of meditation, our body does not release stress chemicals. This state of being promotes a healthy immune system.

You may be curious about achieving these beneficial states of consciousness. There are many methods for producing relaxation and altered states of awareness. The following techniques are offered to assist you.

Meditative Techniques

Sitting Meditation
Create a quiet time and a place where you are in privacy. Sit in a chair or on a pillow on the floor making sure your back is comfortably straight. Select an area of focus such as your breathing or a repeated word (mantra) which appeals to you, such as "peace," "healing," or "love." Allow yourself to fully relax as you close your eyes and focus on your breath or mantra. Each time your mind shifts its attention from your breath or mantra, gently bring it back to your focus.

Continue to meditate on the breath or mantra for as long as you are enjoying the experience and are comfortable. In the beginning you may meditate from one to five minutes. As you practice your meditation time may increase to 20-30 minutes or longer each day. Some people enjoy meditating to soft music or listening to a meditation tape while learning to relax the consciousness. When practiced with respect for yourself and enjoyment as your goal, meditation can be a rewarding part of your day.

Walking Meditation

Walking meditation is ideally practiced in nature, away from other people and the sounds of traffic and civilization. The focus of walking meditation is "mindfulness," being consciously aware of your movement and breath. As you mindfully walk, focus upon your breath. As your mind strays, gently bring your awareness back inside yourself to the breath. This meditation is effective for people who find it difficult to sit quietly for any period of time.

Moving Meditations

Eastern traditional movement exercises such as Yoga, Tai Chi, Aikido and Chi Gong are effective methods of movement meditation. As in other methods of meditation, the focus is inward on the breath and/or energy and movement of the body.

Biofeedback

Biofeedback is an effective tool for assisting the mind to manage the health of the body. Biofeedback is a self-regulating learning process. It is based on receiving feedback from our body on a monitoring machine that registers heart rate or electrical resistance of the skin. A line on a screen or a tone in a headset provides the feedback of bodily functions denoting the user's effectiveness in directing the mind to assist the body. Many people use biofeedback to relieve stress or to manage pain.

Visualization

Visual images are capable of affecting the functioning of our bodies. The messages of the visual images are conveyed throughout the nervous system, the immune system, the organs, muscles, bones and cells of the body. Visual images can communicate feelings in our mind/body that the thinking brain cannot.

Visualization bypasses the rational, left brain and activates the right, healing portions of the brain. When a person visualizes the heart rate slowing down, the heart responds by reducing its rate of beating. Bernie Siegel, M.D., and Drs. Carl and Stephanie Simonton have had tremendous success with cancer patients using visualization techniques. Many of their patients have experienced "spontaneous remissions" where tumors have shrunk or disappeared completely with the use of visualization techniques. Athletes have discovered the power of visualization in sports performance. Visualization is often used as a manifestation tool and for tapping into the right, creative, healing centers of the brain.

There is no "right" or "wrong" way of relaxing and focusing. Trust the technique that feels most suitable for you. The level of enjoyment and effectiveness derived from a given meditative method is the only criterion for selection.

Living in joy promotes the development of optimum health. Health is not an absence of illness, but rather a way of life. Trusting that your mind/body condition is appropriate for you right now contributes to the experience of joy. Joy is the experience of oneness and connectedness in the moment. Pain is the experience of separation from self in the moment. The choice is before us, MOMENT TO MOMENT.

May all things move and be moved in me
and know and be known in me.
May all creation
dance for joy within me.

Chinook Psalter

BE AT PEACE

FOR YOU ARE GREATLY LOVED

7

SACRED AND PROFANE

Be humble for you are made of earth.
Be noble for you are made of stars.

Serbian Proverb

Finding the Sacred Within the Profane

The meaning of "sacred," according to *Webster's Dictionary*, is that which is "entitled to reverence, holy." The definition of "profane" is "to treat (something sacred) with abuse, irreverence or contempt; not holy." In our society the events of our everyday lives are considered unworthy of reverence, unholy. Going to work, driving the car, cooking, cleaning, working on the computer and having conversations are examples of activities considered "mundane." Our bodies, and our sexuality in particular, are frequently viewed with irreverence. Most of our thoughts, feelings and desires are not considered sacred. We profane the ongoing moments of our lives when we limit what is sacred and what is not.

Our lives unfold in moments. When we are not present in those moments, we miss opportunities of transformation and increased awareness. Living fully in the here and now, without imposing anything on it, is a powerful form of mindfulness. Focusing upon each experience in the moment, regardless of the nature of outer circumstances, allows an inner sense of serenity to pervade. It is as if each of us becomes the observer of our own world. We watch ourselves from a peaceful, detached perspective as our awareness grows. From this quiet place within arises the wisdom and insight of our innate intelligence. Deep within us there lives a healthy and trustworthy intuitive core that comes alive as we allow ourselves to be fully present in each moment. It is our entitlement to experience the vast, endless magnificence of total awareness. Life becomes sacred as we are wholly present within each moment of our existence.

Only that day dawns to which we are awake.

Henry David Thoreau, *Walden*

Perhaps living fully in the moment and cultivating an attitude of reverence for all aspects of life are new and challenging to you. You may be inwardly asking yourself, "How do I begin to value, nurture and revere myself in my life? I'm so busy, I don t have time!" *Reverence is an attitude.* Reverence is a tool that assists us in discovering the truth of who we are.

We practice reverence by establishing a loving, accepting attitude toward ourselves much like a loving mother who cherishes a beloved child. We revere ourselves as we access our inner worlds. We choose love as our motivator rather than be incapacitated by our fears. Should we fall out of self-acceptance into fear, we acknowledge our experience and allow our feelings expression, enabling ourselves to operate once again in acceptance and love. We choose to be accountable for our actions and are willing to work on changing the underlying limiting beliefs that keep us stuck. We have the courage to look into the dark places within ourselves and invite our fears into the light of our awareness. These tools provide the foundation upon which to build reverence.

WHEN WE TAKE OURSELVES FOR GRANTED WE PROFANE OURSELVES. WHEN WE RESPECT AND VALUE ALL ASPECTS OF OURSELVES OUR LIVES BECOME SACRED.

EXERCISES TO PROMOTE THE SACRED IN EVERYDAY LIVING

- These exercises offer suggestions for practicing reverence in daily living. Try one or two a day and experiment on your own. The first step is to give yourself *permission* to gradually change your approach to yourself and your life. YOU ARE WORTH IT!

- Upon awakening in the morning, begin your day with an attitude of love for yourself. If you pray, say a prayer invoking a blessing upon yourself and all you love. Hold strong the intention of expressing love for yourself in all that you undertake on this day.

- As you shower/bathe/groom yourself and dress, approach your body in tenderness and appreciation. Wear clothing that feels good to you. Groom your body in a way that sends a message of caring. Touch your body with gentleness and kindness throughout the day.

- Take time to appreciate and/or bless your food before eating. Eat only food that is pleasing and nurturing to you. Take time to enjoy your food. Set your table with care, light a candle and play your favorite music as you eat. Reading or watching television while eating removes you from the present and distracts you from the process of nurturing yourself. Save challenging conversations for another time.

- In the workplace, create a pleasant atmosphere. Place items in view that have personal meaning or that instill warmth, inspiration and pleasure.

- Take time to move your body on a regular basis. Select activities that are enjoyable such as yoga, walking, jogging, swimming, racquetball or aerobics.

- Set aside quiet time daily for relaxation and meditation.

- Participate in at least one fun or relaxing activity a day such as watching a movie, reading, talking and laughing with friends, going for a bicycle ride, playing with children, working with hobbies or crafts.

- Before retiring to bed, reflect upon your day and acknowledge all of the accomplishments and insights you have experienced. If you pray, say a prayer honoring life and yourself. Hold yourself in love as you fall asleep.

Approaching life in a respectful manner establishes momentum for creating the sacred within the profane. As you practice these and other methods of honoring yourself, the lives of those around you will be affected as well. The world will soon reflect your belief in the deep integrity of your own being. There will be something distinctive about you to which other people will be attracted.

The love and appreciation we feel for ourselves radiates outward and draws to us those who love and appreciate us too. Their ability to love and appreciate themselves is strengthened in our presence. Love is contagious.

Once you have established yourself as a center of love and
kindness radiating through your being, which amounts
to a cradling of yourself in loving kindness and acceptance,
you can dwell here indefinitely, drinking at this fount,
bathing in it, renewing yourself, nourishing yourself,
enlivening yourself.

Jon Kabat-Zinn, Ph. D., *Wherever You Go There You Are*

An often overlooked aspect contributing to the sacred in life is the observance of change and transitional passages. Change is not easily received by many of us. We frequently ignore change in an effort to avoid the challenging conditions that accompany the transitions of our lives.

Marking the Passages of Life

INSIGHT IS THE GIFT OF CHANGE. TRUE WISDOM IS
FOUND IN THE VOYAGES OF TRANSITION.

In our Western culture we have a fairly rigid set of occasions we celebrate: birthdays, weddings, anniversaries, funerals and holidays. Celebration rituals for life-changing events such as divorce, the onset of puberty, entering adulthood and menopause have been lost to antiquity. Divorce is generally viewed as an ending; it is rarely celebrated as a beginning. Graduation from high school or college is a rite of passage into adulthood. Seldom does this celebration serve to honor the emotional transition of leaving childhood and entering the new world of responsible adulthood. While a funeral honors the deceased, rarely does it honor the different directions the survivors' lives will take. The purposes of many of our holidays have been lost to indifference and commercialization.

In some cultures the passage into puberty is honored for both boys and girls. In our culture the onset of menstruation is often shrouded in secrecy, ignorance and embarrassment. The monthly cycle is referred to by some as being "on the rag" or "the curse." As boys approach puberty they frequently explore their emerging sexuality through locker room conversations, lewd humor and the investigation of "X-rated" magazines and books. Will it be possible for these emerging young men and women to develop a sense of reverence for their own and others' bodies? We profane our bodies in our culture with the prevalence of shame-producing sexual attitudes.

Any change that occurs on one level of our lives automatically affects other levels of our experience. A shift in our spirituality affects our emotional, mental and physical well-being. A physical change such as moving to a new home, starting a new job, beginning a new relationship, having a child, moving into mid-life, affects us on other levels—emotional, mental and spiritual. As we pause to observe these life passages, we grant ourselves the understanding that is necessary to gracefully transition change. Unless we take time to honor our life passages, they are profaned.

A ritual is a ceremony that is performed with the intent of honoring and defining transitions in life. Personal ritual provides a powerful, practical way to capture the emotional energy that accompanies transition throughout life's journeys. When practiced with an attitude of reverence and respect, ritual provides the means to transform the profane to the sacred.

Creating Rituals

The observance of a special event does not require expense, time or elaborate trappings. Keeping it simple is the most effective approach. The *attitude* that you bring to your celebration ritual is of most importance. All who participate with you will feel nurtured, respected and honored when the ritual is centered from the heart. Utilizing one or more of the four natural elements of water, fire, air and earth adds impact and resonates with meaning for most of us. A candle may be used for introducing the element of fire into ritual, a feather for air, rocks/crystals/sand for the earth element and a special container for water.

The following are examples for personal ritual:

- A young woman entering puberty is presented with a rose and her favorite dinner, lit by candlelight. During dinner she and others present are encouraged to share their feeings and thoughts about this special time in her life.

- A friend is ending a relationship. To commemorate the ending of her relationship and the beginning of a new way of life, she uses water as a symbol of "washing away and cleansing" the ended relationship (the source of water may take the form of a special trip to the ocean, favorite lake, river or stream, fountain or by using a simple bowl of water). As she applies water to her body, she focuses on letting go of the old and allowing a new sense of love and peace to fill her. To signify the emergence of new life, she plants a tree or flower to complete her transition ritual.

• A young man is graduating from college. In observance of leaving childhood and entering into the role of an adult, he gathers a group of male friends and relatives to share a campfire outing. At the campfire, each person assembled gives the young man a verbal "gift of confidence," voicing his unique gifts and capabilities. One of the men records the verbal gifts and presents them to him as a keepsake in a wood-framed mounting.

A special passage in life is most effectively celebrated with simplicity, creativity and an attitude of respect that accompanies an open heart. Rituals that include dance, drumming, music and the four elements bypass the busy, thinking cortex of the left brain functions and register deeply in the brain centers associated with emotion and regulation of the body (right brain functions). Ritual provides the means to communicate *directly* with the healing portion of the brain.

Symbols play an important role in formulating rituals. Symbols are part of our daily existence. The language of symbols is used every night as we dream. Beautiful young women with sex appeal are often used as symbols by advertisers to promote their products. A flag is a symbol of a nation's pride and unity.

Symbols are part of history, religion and education—they are in every aspect of life. Rituals and their symbols are unique expressions of our individual needs, perspectives and aspirations. No *Manual for Correct Rituals and Their Symbols* exists. The use of symbols that evoke feelings of love and empowerment assist the profound sense of personal change that accompanies ritual. The color green may be worn to denote healing, planting seeds may represent new growth, a rose may symbolize beauty and love, dancing may enact vigor and life, drumming may signify connection to spirit, water may characterize purification and cleansing. The colors, sounds, movement and physical symbols of ritual assist us in moving through our experiences to connect us to our inner selves.

Ritual is an effective tool for transition through challenging circumstances; however, it will not magically transform a bad situation into a good one. The changes required to move through challenge usually require time. All challenge carries the potential gift of growth. When we walk through challenge and embrace it with ritual, fear dissolves into courage. We gain wisdom, self-esteem and self-trust as we successfully pass through life's struggles. Ritual supplies a powerful tool for transition.

RITUAL ASSISTS US IN THE COMPLETION OF EXPERIENCES AND EMOTIONS. IT PROVIDES AVENUES FOR SHIFTING FROM THE INTELLECTUAL PURSUITS OF THE LEFT BRAIN INTO THE CREATIVE POWER OF THE RIGHT BRAIN. RITUAL SUPPORTS HEALING AND INTEGRATION INTO OUR WHOLENESS.

Left and Right Brain Activity

Science has divided the brain into two functioning catagories—the left and right hemispheres. (These are not necessarily physical localities within the brain, but rather predominate traits.) The *left hemisphere* is the place where conscious, rational, analytical thought resides. Within the left brain reason, words and practical, intellectual, logical pursuits are born. The *right hemisphere* houses creativity, imagination and an affinity for nurturing. Access to our intuition, emotions, spirituality, power and healing is provided by the right brain. It is the connection to our creativity and the feeling center of the heart.

Our culture has historically placed great value on the rational, analytical left brain processes and has devalued the intuitive, emotional workings of the right brain. Intuition is a product of right brain activity, and until recently, has been considered a process of the "emotional female" creature. Today, there is fresh appreciation for intuitive capabilities as evidenced by books, classes and seminars featuring development of the right brain function of intuition.

Intuitive practices are rapidly becoming a part of daily life as business people (both male and female) learn to rely on their "hunches" and "gut feelings." For example, a successful stockbroker may utilize logical information (left brain thinking) as well as a highly developed intuitive sense (right brain). Many inventions and scientific discoveries have resulted from the intuitive process. Einstein and Edison took numerous catnaps throughout the day, setting aside the left brain processes and turning to intuition for their inspiration. Einstein declared "I have not arrived at my understanding of the universe by means of the rational mind." Intuition has come into its own as a viable human resource.

Total reliance upon the limited information accessed by the analytical, intellectual left brain leaves us literally wandering in the dark. The logical, left brain relies solely upon and is limited by the perceptions of the five senses and its own reasoning capabilities. With the right brain, however, we are granted an unlimited spectrum of knowledge and information. The right brain has the capability to tap into the deep inner realms of the unconscious where our intuition resides.

Intuition provides information that the logical, left brain is unable to access. The right brain operates outside of the parameters of the perception of the five senses. It is the quiet, still, inner voice. Intuition allows us admission to the higher nature of ourselves and our universe. As we open to the intuitive functions of the right brain, we expand into unlimited potential. We live in rhythm with ourselves and our world. We experience our wholeness.

The left brain serves us by performing an essential function. It filters all of the information that we perceive from our inner and outer worlds. The left brain creates order out of the ceaseless flow of data with which we are inundated. Ideally we *balance* right brain activity with left brain resources. From this place of balance, we are enabled to realize our greatest aspirations in life.

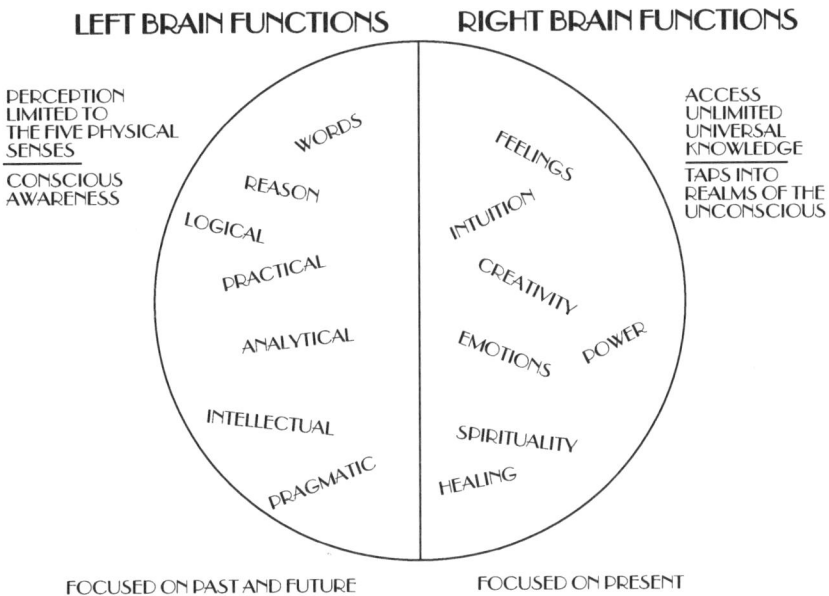

LEFT BRAIN FUNCTIONS   RIGHT BRAIN FUNCTIONS

PERCEPTION LIMITED TO THE FIVE PHYSICAL SENSES

CONSCIOUS AWARENESS

ACCESS UNLIMITED UNIVERSAL KNOWLEDGE

TAPS INTO REALMS OF THE UNCONSCIOUS

WORDS
REASON
LOGICAL
PRACTICAL
ANALYTICAL
INTELLECTUAL
PRAGMATIC

FEELINGS
INTUITION
CREATIVITY
EMOTIONS   POWER
SPIRITUALITY
HEALING

FOCUSED ON PAST AND FUTURE   FOCUSED ON PRESENT

Ariana's Partnering of the Left and Right Brain

When Ariana needed some new bedroom furniture, she did what most people do when they desire something new—she went shopping (left brain activity). She went to several stores and saw numerous sets of bedroom furniture, none of which appealed to her. Still, she wanted very much to redecorate, so she decided to meditate about it (right brain activity).

In her meditation she intuitively "saw" (visualization—right brain) a scene right out of the "Arabian Nights" for her bedroom! In her vision she pictured a beautiful, sheer drape hanging from the ceiling encircling a very low, pedestal bed adorned with many lovely pillows. A large oriental carpet completed the scene. That was it; there was no other furniture in the room.

Once she had envisioned what she wanted, she understood why she couldn't find anything she liked in the furniture stores! However, Ariana went shopping once more, this time with a definite plan in mind (left brain). She found the oriental rug right away, but the real challenge lay in creating the rest of the Arabian Nights scene. Where would she find the sheer draping to surround her bed, the elegant, over-sized pillows, the unusual bed and platform? She wasn't even sure what size the bed should be—twin? double? queen? king? To find the answer she tried muscle testing (right brain—see note below), but "none of the above" was the answer she received.

(Note: Muscle testing is a means by which the body's reflexes can be used to gain access to information which is stored in the mind/body. The muscle is an energy circuit indicator.)

A bedding store owner, unable to assist her, referred her to an interior decorator (left brain). The decorator came to Ariana's house, looked at her bedroom and immediately announced, "You need a three-quarter-sized mattress." Once that piece of the puzzle was solved, the decorator was able to help Ariana create the rest of the "Arabian Nights scene she had envisioned.

Ariana's bedroom is now the manifestation of the intuitive vision she received that day in meditation. It is beautiful and magical! Her bedroom came into being through the partnership of the left and right brain processes.

It is important to note that the left brain focuses primarily on the *past* and *future* while the right brain focuses on the *present*. When we are planning for the future or reliving the past, we are focused in left brain functioning. As we focus in the present moment, we live in right brain activity. Our focus on past/future or present can serve as a reminder as to which hemisphere of the brain we are accessing in the moment.

As young children we lived primarily in the right side of the brain. Our lives were filled with imagination, creativity and fun! By the time we reached the first grade, our social conditioning began which taught us to rely more and more on the rational, analytical thinking processes of the left brain. For most of us, with time, the left brain took on a dominant role with society's emphasis and encouragement for rational, analytical and intellectual pursuits.

How can we build upon our connection to the right brain and regain the magic and wonder of life?

The Magical Tool in Life—INTUITION

It is only with the heart that one can see rightly; what is essential is invisible to the eye.

Antoine De Saint-Exupery, *The Little Prince*

Webster's Dictionary defines intuition as "the power or faculty of attaining direct knowledge or cognition without rational thought and inference—quick and ready insight." Intuition is a seemingly magical process as insight and instantaneous knowing appear out of nowhere without effort on our part.

Each person possesses a unique way of receiving intuitive information. The manner in which the intuitive information is received may vary from circumstance to circumstance in an individual's life. Some people *see* visual pictures in their mind's eye, other people *hear* inner messages or music, others receive *thoughts* out of the blue while others *feel* sensations in their bodies, such as chills when they encounter information that rings true.

There are four primary vehicles which provide access to the right brain's intuitive functions:

1. Physical Body
2. Feelings/Emotions
3. Thoughts/Words
4. Visualization/Imagery

1. Physical Body

Paying close attention to the sensations of our physical bodies opens the possibilities for us to gain intuitive insight.

We are a mind/body system which houses intelligence in every cell. The following examples, as well as other physical sensations of discomfort, are intuitive bodily warnings signaling that there are areas out of alignment: my stomach aches every time I am in the presence of a particular person, my head begins to throb the moment I enter my place of work, I feel nauseous when I am looking down from high elevations. When we pay attention, our bodies "speak" to us through feeling sensation.

Our bodies also register intuitive signals of pleasure. My heart flutters and leaps for joy when I encounter my lover. I whistle a cheerful tune as I head for work every day. My eyes well up with tears of appreciation when I hear a moving piece of music or view a scene of immense beauty. These are examples of intuitive physical sensations registering harmony, well-being and pleasure in our world. Messages concerning our inner state of well-being are registered in our conscious minds through the process of intuitive body signals.

2. Feelings/Emotions

Intuitive information comes to us through our feelings and emotions. For example, I feel elated and expectant without the conscious understanding of why I am having such an upbeat experience. I feel uneasy and apprehensive about my encounter with a stranger on the bus this morning. I have a sense of dread as I go for my job interview. I walk out of the seminar I have just completed with happiness and excitement.

Until the "why I feel this way," (the reasons and underlying sources of my feelings) becomes apparent, I could easily doubt my feelings. After all, there is no logical (left brain) reason why I should feel the way I do in any of the above examples.

The intelligence of the unconscious offers us access to its contents through the intuitive feeling process.

3. Thoughts/Words

Intuitive messages frequently appear as thoughts and words appearing unexpectedly in our minds. They often accompany other intuitive functions such as intuitive physical body sensations, feelings/emotions and visions. These words or thoughts resonate as *truth* as we receive them, and we are filled with an inner certainty that possesses no available, logical explanation.

4. Visualization/Imagery

Visualization and imagery provide mechanisms to receive and guide our intuition. The messages of dreams are a product of intuition at work through visualization and imagery. In focused visualization practices, such as those used for healing purposes, our intuition is put to work through bypassing the left brain and drawing on right brain resources. In meditation, visual images that appear to us come from the deep inner intuitive portions of our beings. Imaginary visions that occur in daydreams frequently carry messages of an intuitive nature that could not be accessed through our busy, thinking left brains.

The visualization aspect of the intuitive process is often a subtle, yet persistent visual attraction to a particular item or person. We are drawn visually by our intuitive knowing. An encounter Annaliese had illustrates this point vividly. Her husband, David, spent the greater part of one day frantically looking through paperwork in his office for a bid he had prepared for a contractor. Each time she entered his office, he would comment, "I'm still looking for that bid." His secretary had joined him in his futile search throughout the day but was unable to help.

At seven that evening, David was still at his office where Annaliese found him consumed in his search for the lost bid. While chatting with him as he looked through yet another pile of file folders, her attention was drawn to a particular file folder on his secretary's desk (the working of her visual, intuitive process). She told herself, "No, they must have already looked in that file. It's in plain sight." (Her reasoning, logical left brain took over). While she spoke with David, her attention was repeatedly drawn to the same file in his secretary's file holder (her visual intuitive process still attempting to get her attention). Finally Annaliese picked up the file folder, opened it, held it up for David to inspect and asked, "Is this the bid?" He cried, "Yes!" As this example demonstrates, our intuitive intelligence is available for accessing unlimited information, including the whereabouts of lost articles should we choose to pay attention to it.

Can we trust our intuition? Can we grant it validity? It is commonplace to shrug off intuitive messages with "I probably imagined it" or "I must have been dreaming." The way to determine whether a piece of intuitive information is reliable is to look at the results in our lives. When we are in harmony with our intuitive natures, doors of insight and opportunity open readily for us. Life flows easily as we connect with our intuition, trusting its validity and acting upon its messages.

Our intuition attempts to caution us about potential areas of difficulty. Beneficial choices are revealed to us through intuitive communication registered as feelings, thoughts or visual images resonating as *truth* in our bodies. The more valuable choice or decision will produce feelings of warmth, certainty and a sense of rightness in our beings. If we are not paying attention to our intuitive messages and proceed with a choice out of harmony with our highest good, we will experience feelings of anxiety, distress and confusion within our mind/bodies.

An intuitive vision, feeling, thought or sensation suddenly comes to us. What to do? Learning to act on these intuitive messages requires cultivating the skill of discernment. This is where calling upon the intellectual capabilities of the left brain becomes important. The rational, thinking left brain's job, so to speak, is to make sense of the information we receive, including intuitive input.

Suppose Susan, while grocery shopping, notices a sick feeling in her stomach accompanied by the thought "My boyfriend is going to break up with me." Chills run down her back. Her intuitive gut feeling is subtle, yet insistent. Now Susan is at a choice point. She can dismiss these feelings and message with "It's just my imagination," or she can follow them up by putting her rational, left brain to work and taking appropriate action.

She takes a moment to think about her recent experiences with her boyfriend (putting her left brain to work). She recalls that he has been withdrawn recently, making excuses to break dates with her. Susan decides to meet with her boyfriend. Upon sharing her revelations with her boyfriend, he concedes that he had been considering ending their relationship. Although Susan was not pleased with this confirmation, she felt a sense of relief in knowing the truth. Most importantly, she felt empowered in trusting and following her intuition. Armed with the certainty of possessing a reliable internal resource (her intuition), her transition from her relationship was not as traumatic as it would have been without these resources.

Trusting our intuition requires taking risks. We risk making a mistake in discerning the truth about a situation. We risk looking foolish to others and ourselves. We risk changing ourselves, our relationships, our health and our environment. We risk discovering a greater level of satisfaction in life through the use of our inner resources. We risk becoming powerful decision-makers and taking assertive action based on these decisions. Yes, there are risks.

Ariana's Story

A few years ago, Ariana became aware of her fears and judgments about being late for engagements and appointments. She held a strong expectation about being on time. She had a conversation with this fear of being late, inviting it into her circle of light (awareness). She intuitively received the understanding that "she will always be where she is supposed to be at exactly the right time." This means that there may be times when she arrives earlier than the agreed upon time, and instances where she may arrive later than the appointed time, and other times when she will arrive at exactly the time agreed upon. Regardless, she will always arrive at the *right time.*

She now trusts her intuitive inner guidance to direct her to be where she is supposed to be, when she is supposed to be, with whom she is supposed to be, acting and speaking in an appropriate manner. Does this mean that all of her fears and judgments have disappeared regarding punctuality? No! It means that each time her fears and judgments arise she addresses them by enlisting the aid of her intuitive awareness.

TRUST IN OUR INTUITIVE INTELLIGENCE LEADS US TO BE IN THE RIGHT PLACE AT THE RIGHT TIME.

Our intuitive voice works quietly, discreetly and patiently, unlike the critical voice discussed in Chapter Four. The voice of intuition does not invoke guilt or make demands. It is as subtle and gentle as a soft breeze—we can miss it entirely by not focusing on our present experience.

An intuitive message makes its way to us while we are relaxed. Messages do not necessarily appear while meditating or during visualization. Our efforts to receive a message can promote stress and remove us from the open, relaxed state necessary to hear the still, quiet voice of intuition. The voice of intuition often makes itself known while undertaking every-day tasks, such as making the bed, washing the car, driving, exercising, brushing our teeth and so on. Intuitive messages are received only when we are relaxed and present. Intuition rarely appears in the same company as stress.

*Relaxation is the body's way of surrendering
to the moment.*

Dan Millman, *The Laws of Spirit*

We are able to access our intuitive capabilities when:
   (1) we are focused in the present moment (right brain)
   (2) we are in a relaxed, open state (right brain)

Intuitive messages often appear outside of ourselves through someone or something in our world. Coincidences, synchronistic occurrences and patterns in life are frequently offered as intuitive messages. Paying attention to the occur-rences around us (living in the present moment) and being open and relaxed are requirements for receiving messages from the world at large.

For example, let us say that a friend has been trying to deliver a message of importance to me for months. I have been hearing the message but tuning it out, justifying my action with "It's just my friend talking." Then one day I happen to read a book that carries the exact message that my friend has been giving me but this time I am open to receiving it! In another instance, I turn on the television and a program that offers insights into a problem area in my life appears on the screen, or I may overhear a conversation that provides a solution for which I have been searching. The world is full of messages if we pay attention. Intuition will point us in the direction of these messages and assist us in interpreting and verifying the meaning. Our reasoning capabilities (left brain) assist us to trust the messages and follow through with appropriate actions.

Intuition is the highest uncluttered part of ourselves speaking from our greatest knowing.

David R. Hagan

EXERCISE: USING THE INTUITION FOR PROBLEM SOLVING

Clearly state the nature of a problem you would like resolved on paper. Limit your focus to one problem at a time.

Option One

Before going to sleep, ask your unconscious to provide a dream containing the information you need to solve your problem. Use clear intention to program your conscious mind to remember the contents of your dream by stating: "Unconscious, I intend to consciously recall the contents of the dream which will assist me in resolving my problem." Upon awakening, record the details of your dream(s). Repeat your request until the dream is provided that solves your dilemma.

Option Two

Sit in a relaxed position with your back comfortably straight. Bring the problem or situation you are facing to mind. Ask the unconscious for a solution: "Unconscious, I am willing to receive the understanding and insights that convey the solution to my problem." Simply focus on your breath and relax. Allow your mind to be still, trusting that the solution will be provided through your open awareness. Continue to breathe and relax. Let go of any tension held in your body. Allow your mind to be totally present in this moment, focusing only on the breath. Pay attention to mental pictures that occur, thoughts that come to mind, physical bodily sensations or feelings of emotion that arise within you in this relaxed, focused state. These are the vehicles used for communication by the intuition. After receiving a message from the intuition, notice if there is a sense of well-being, or is there a growing feeling of anxiousness and confusion? The intuitive response will resonate with a feeling of harmony and certainty in your mind/body. Trust your heart to feel and your mind to discern the truth of your intuitive message.

As we open ourselves to explore our intuitive channels, life becomes vital, creative, reliable and adventurous. With practice the intuition can assist us in all decision making in matters large and small—what food to eat, what to wear, where to live, what work to perform, when to speak and what to say, how to spend our time, how to create health, and so on. Intention, persistence and trust in our inner knowing (our intuition) will provide openings into new areas of effectiveness in living. In this endeavor, we move out of the profane and into the sacred.

Following the Passions of Our Hearts— Our True Nature

Following the passion of our hearts means responding authentically to our thoughts, feelings and experiences—living in our truth. As children we did this naturally until we became socially conditioned. Many of us learned at an early age that to be accepted and loved, we had to stifle our authentic selves and adopt the "nice boy/nice girl" persona that was expected of us. We buried the truth of our authentic selves in order to win approval. It seemed our very survival was dependent upon pleasing the all-powerful and important people of our world.

Beneath the masks we presented to the world, our true natures lay hidden and dormant. We stifled our spontaneity, opinions, desires, angers, fears, joys and sorrows. With time we began to forget who we truly were and started to believe that we were the personalities and the masks of approval we took on early in life. Life becomes devoid of meaning in this loss of self.

We are capable of reclaiming these natural responses to our experiences and passions. The truth of who we are never dies. It remains alive within us seeking expression. Many of us have hidden the truth of ourselves under layers of conditioning, practical day-to-day routine and, ultimately, fear. Truth lives in the shadows when it is not realized. Discovering our authentic nature is most effectively pursued through intuitive, right brain functions.

Fears may appear as you delve into and explore your hidden characteristics, dreams, desires and passions. This is a time to cultivate compassion for yourself. In this endeavor you are literally stripping away old, protected and cherished patterns and beliefs. They will not want to die easily or quietly. When fear is encountered in this process, you may take it into your circle of light (awareness) and begin an inner dialogue to ascertain its needs. (See the guided visualization exercise from Chapter Five.) This process can be repeated many times, revealing new and different information each time. Inviting the unknown elements of ourselves into the realm of our consciousness changes their status from stranger, cloaked in darkness to friend surrounded by acceptance and light.

Only by our living fully in our truth are our inner and outer worlds in harmony. Inner and outer harmony promotes the manifestation of healing and wholeness. In following our light, our actions flow naturally and freely from our inner convictions. Life takes on renewed meaning as the love and acceptance of our true nature comes forth.

Intuition: Source of Creativity and Well-Being

The child within us awakens as we follow the passions of our hearts. Our creative outlets are opened when we trust our intuitive intelligence to guide us in resolving problems and expressing our innate talents and capabilities. It is easy to become caught up in the details of our hectic lives, ignoring the importance of creative expression. Expressing our creativity provides the outlet for enhancing our emotional and physical health. For many of us creative outlets are not only enjoyable, but mandatory for our well-being. The following story illustrates the importance of following our creative passions. It has been paraphrased from the book *The Wizdom Within.*

A hard-working, no-nonsense corporate CEO worked hard and built a successful, profitable business. He thought he was doing well except for his tendency to throw temper tantrums. When it became apparent that these outbursts were alienating his employees and disrupting his marriage, he decided to control his tendency to rant and rave the way he did everything else in life—he simply stifled it. As a result of stuffing his feelings, he developed a deep suicidal depression for which he was hospitalized.

In the hospital it was discovered that he was an art school graduate who loved to paint. Through the years he had sacrificed his creativity to make money and climb the corporate ladder. He suppressed his urge to paint because he believed that "doing what you like to do just because it makes you feel good is a waste of time since it does not produce income." He was put in an art therapy program, his depression disappeared, and he was released from the hospital.

Upon returning to his normal life, he gave up painting. Within eighteen months he was back in the hospital with suicidal depression, which again lifted completely in art therapy. After undergoing a third cycle of suicidal depression, hospitalization and art therapy, he consulted the author of *The Wizdom Within*. While telling his story, he experienced a powerful insight: "setting aside two or three hours every day to vent his urge to paint would be much more cost effective than spending a month or two in the sanitarium every couple of years."

This man's life was transformed when he was able to shift his belief from "doing something you feel like doing just because you feel like doing it is self-indulgent, a waste of time, and without value," to an appreciation of the value of creative pursuits. With this important shift in his beliefs, he was able to permit himself a pleasurable creative outlet which supported him in remaining emotionally and mentally stable and healthy.

OUR LIVES ARE EITHER FOCUSED ON:
THE PURSUIT OF JOY—MOTIVATED BY LOVE
(MOVING TOWARD WHAT WE WANT.)
OR
THE AVOIDANCE OF PAIN—MOTIVATED BY FEAR
(TRYING TO ESCAPE WHAT WE DO NOT WANT.)

Which of these motivators have you been allowing to influence your life—the avoidance of pain or the pursuit of joy? It is evident which of these motivators is health-producing and which is debilitating. Can you rearrange your life's focus to include the pursuit of creative outlets?

EXERCISE: PLEASURABLE CREATIVE OUTLETS

Step One
Take a few moments to relax and focus. Make a list of everything you love to do but seldom get around to doing—dancing, painting, singing, hiking, meditating, gardening, cooking, skating, handicrafts, building models, running through the sprinkler—the list can be endless. Stop writing when the flow of ideas ends.

Step Two
Choose the three top items from your list that are your favorites—activities that, when you imagine doing them, you smile inwardly with anticipated pleasure. Trust your intuition to assist you in making your choices.

Step Three

Commit to a specific time frame when you will gift yourself with fully enjoying your top three activities! This time frame need not be time intensive. Perhaps, one of your top three activities is reading romance novels. How often and for how long will you set aside time to read—ten minutes every day, one solid hour once a week, maybe twenty minutes three times a week. Be very clear about your time commitment. Write your time commitment next to each of your selected items. (If resistance and reasons to avoid this exercise come up during this step, refer back to the "Shifting Beliefs Exercise" in Chapter Two.)

Step Four

Follow through by doing what you commit to do. Enlist the support of a trusted friend or loved one to assist you in stepping out of your comfort zone and pursuing the pleasurable activities that enrich your well-being. The simple act of sharing your commitment with another person is often motivation enough to follow through with your game plan. Let them know how they can assist you. Would you feel supported if they call you once a week to hear a report on how you are doing with your commitment, or would you prefer to meet with them regularly over a cup of coffee to discuss your progress? It is important to create a sense of pleasure in your relationship with your support partners.

If one advances confidently in the direction of his dreams, and endeavors to live the life which he has imagined, he will meet with a success unexpected in common hours.

Henry David Thoreau

Living from the passion of our hearts is an exciting, ever-changing, life-long gift. In honoring our authentic, passionate nature, we elevate ourselves from the profane to the sacred. There is no final destination in this undertaking; rather, it is a rich, full experience that comes from returning to our true nature. As we approach our journey with a sense of pleasant anticipation and adventure, we progress in a state of well-being, harmony and joy! We come home.

BE AT PEACE

FOR YOU ARE GREATLY LOVED

8

COMING HOME

Our deepest fear is not that we are inadequate. Our deepest fear is that we are powerful beyond all measure. It is our light, not our darkness, that most frightens us....

Marianne WIlliamson, *A Return to Love*
Quoted in the 1994 inaugural speech
of President Nelson Mandela

Balance and Peace

We have traveled far and wide in our journey into wholeness, and now we are ready to return home. What is waiting for us at home? The truth is we are always home in our true nature, no matter where we venture. When we journey into wholeness, we return to our inner center of calm, balance and peace, more enriched and expanded. Our inherent nature is perfection—this is our HOME.

In our center which is our home, there is no separation, no duality, no polarity, only oneness with all that we are. We are integrated, whole and at peace, with all of our systems in alignment and working together. When we live in the moment, embracing all aspects of ourselves, we rise above the limitations of fear and expand into the center of calm which exists in the eye of the storm. This center is our true nature, our point of power and balance. Peace is the result of living in our home. We walk with certainty in the truth of who we are and realize our wholeness.

Above the doorway to Apollo's Temple at Delphi in Greece was this inscription: "Know Thyself." Knowing ourselves in our divine, true nature is powerfully liberating and lays the foundation for a life of self-mastery.

We have become adept at focusing on our shortcomings, our imperfections and our failures. We possess so much more breadth and depth than believed possible for "mere humans." The veils of unawareness can cloud the vision of our inner light, making it appear as though we live in density and darkness. It is as if we have developed tunnel vision which allows us to perceive only the slightest glimpse of our innate essence, leaving the ultimate truth of our brilliance unobserved.

Our darkness is an illusion—we are the personification of all that is resplendent! Just as thick layers of clouds hide the light of the sun, the truth of our inner nature has been hidden and awaits its unveiling. Our challenge is to remove the blinders we have placed upon ourselves and gather the courage to perceive the vastness and infinitude within our very heart and soul.

As Nelson Mandela so eloquently stated in his 1994 inaugural speech, "We are brilliant, gorgeous, talented and fabulous." (See Chapter One.) This frightens us. We are afraid of our magnificence, our power, our light. "What will other people think? Will I fit in? What will happen to me if I acknowledge my brilliance?" Beauty exists in everyone, as President Mandela says, and by hiding our light we do not "serve the world." It is by living in our true nature of beauty, joy, peace, balance and love that we give others "permission to do the same." By claiming our true selves, we become whole—we are at home.

Unfolding the truth of our existence is a life-long process, the ultimate core of a spiritually-centered life. In the deep, still, quiet recesses of the human heart lives the hunger to savor the beauty, power and magnitude that comprise our sublime nature. To the degree we give credence to our inherent power and perfection, we live in peace, abundance, fulfillment, love and joy.

This, dear friends, is what the journey of life is about— awakening to the truth of who we are. There is no grander undertaking than this.

And did you get what you
wanted from this life, even so?
I did.
And what did you want?
To call myself beloved, to feel myself
beloved on the earth.

Raymond Carver, *Late Fragment*

BE AT PEACE

FOR YOU ARE GREATLY LOVED

IN CLOSING....

This book was written out of a deep love for humanity, love for ourselves and from the calling within our souls. We both have been interested in all levels of well-being for many years. Out of our eagerness and passion for sharing our acquired insights, we were inspired to make available the information offered in *Journey Into Wholeness.* We were not sure at the onset which medium to work through: videos, seminars, or a book? One day after meditating together, Annaliese announced, "Let's write a book!"

Our intuitions provided the means for acquiring the title and subtitle. The chapter titles were received in a meditation together. The book cover design was shown to us one day soon after we had begun our work together. A reflection of light appeared on the ground outside Annaliese's home. There is no logical, left brain explanation as to how or why the symbol of light appeared. We took pictures of it and gave them to our artist friend, Stephen Peringer. He creatively brought to fruition the profound piece of artwork on the cover of *Journey Into Wholeness.* This symbol inspired us throughout the writing of the book.

Journey Into Wholeness has come into existence as if by magic. We have been supported by those of the seen and the unseen world every step of the way. We took time to honor each step with small ceremonies: toasting with a glass of homemade elderberry wine, sharing a celebratory meal, lighting a candle and hiking to the top of our special mountain.

Each time we sat down to write, we attuned ourselves to our intuition and made a spiritual connection with each other (we live about 365 miles apart). We wrote only two hours a day as mentioned earlier, took extended time off for vacations and other commitments and completed our book within a year's time.

Writing this book presented both of us with the opportunity to continue working on our unresolved issues and to claim greater levels of ownership of our true natures. It is not just coincidence that, as we wrote about specific topics, issues presented themselves for resolution in our lives. We have grown and evolved far beyond where we were when we started this venture. We continue to grow and evolve. This is how we journey into wholeness.

BE AT PEACE

FOR YOU ARE GREATLY LOVED!

A Note From the Authors

You can contribute to the growing collection of knowledge that supports us in realizing our wholeness by writing to us. Please share your insights and personal experiences about applying the concepts presented in *Journey Into Wholeness*. Your personal accounts are valuable.

It would give us great pleasure to assist you personally in your *Journey Into Wholeness*. Weekend *Journey Into Wholeness* workshops and week-long retreats will soon be available. Information about workshops and retreats may be obtained by writing us:

JOURNEY INTO WHOLENESS
P.O. Box 5966
Lynnwood, Washington 98046

(Include self-addressed, stamped envelope.)

References

Bly, Robert. *A Little Book On The Human Shadow.* San Francisco, CA: Harper, 1988.

Chopra, Deepak, M.D. *Quantum Healing.* New York, NY: Bantam Books, 1990.

Duff, Kat. *The Alchemy of Illness.* New York, NY: Bell Tower, 1993.

Kabat-Zinn, Jon. *Wherever You Go, There you Are.* New York, NY: Hyperion, 1994.

Maddi, Salvatore & Kobasa, Suzanne. *The Hardy Executive.* Chicago, IL: Dorsey Professional Books, 1984.

Moyers, Bill. *Healing and the Mind.* Public Affairs Television, Inc., Public Television Series, 1993.

Moyers, Bill. *Healing and the Mind.* New York, NY: Doubleday, 1993.

Rychlak, Joseph F. *Introduction To Personality and Psychotherapy.* Boston, MA: Houghton Mifflin Company, 1981.

Sanbek, Terence J. *The Deadly Diet.* Oakland, CA: New Harbinger Publications, Inc., 1993.

The Institute of Noetic Sciences with William Poole. *The Heart of Healing.* Atlanta, GA: Turner Publishing, Inc., 1993.

Whitfield, Charles, M.D. *Boundaries and Relationships.* Deerfield Beach, FL: Health Communications, Inc., 1993.

Winter, Theresa. *Intuitions.* West Chester, PA: Whitford Press, 1988.

ORDER FORM

Qty.	Title	Price	Can. Price	Total
	JOURNEY INTO WHOLENESS	**$12.95**	**$15.95**	
	Shipping and handling (add $3.00 for first book, $2.00 for each additonal book)			
	Sales tax (WA residents only, add 8.2%)			
	Total enclosed			

Telephone Orders:
Call (800) 461-1931
Have your VISA or
MasterCard ready.

Fax Orders:
(206) 672-8597
Fill out order
blank and fax.

Postal Orders:
Hara Publishing
P.O. Box 19732
Seattle, WA 98109

Payment:Please Check One

☐ Check

☐ VISA

☐ MasterCard

Expiration Date:_____ / _____

Card #:_____

Name on Card:_____

Name_____

Address_____

City_____ State_____ Zip_____

Daytime Phone(_____) _____

Quantity discounts are available.
For more information, call (206) 672-8597.

Thank you for your order!

I understand that I may return any books
for a full refund if not satisfied